S.M.I.L.E.

FOR SUCCESS

*With the Support
of Your People*

JIM DREHER

ISBN-13: 978-1495393723
ISBN-10: 1495393720

For

Cody, Jared Jr., Darren, Cambria,
and your future children.

Dedicated to Kathy

My best friend and married partner in life,
who each day blesses everyone
with the gifts of her positive attitude,
selfless giving, and loving heart.

CONTENTS

Acknowledgments xi

Introduction xiii

    Why This Book?... xiii
    Why This Design?.. xvi
    Why Your People?... xviii

1. Select Your Attitude...1

Attitude of Choice...4

    Everything is a Choice 4
    Choose Your Response... 5
    Stories on Choice 6
        Tough Decisions 7
        Cause, Not Effect..8
        The Best 10
    Reflect on Choice... 13

Attitude of Purpose 14

    Doer 16
    Smiler.. 18
    Solver.. 20
    Victor.. 23
    Stories on Purpose 25
        One Purpose 25
        Many Purposes..26
        Problem Architect...30
        Problem Solved..31
    Reflect on Purpose.. 32

Attitude of Possibility...33

    Possibility Blockers 34
    Possibility Zone.. 36
        Self-Talk 37
        Visualization 39
        Affirmations 42
        Reticular Activating System..45
        Uncomfortable Zone..46
        Wizards...48

Stories on Possibility 49

    Teaching Without a Voice...49

    You Get What You Inspect...51

    Chuck-A-Puck..53

    Musical Imperfection 54

    No Regrets...55

Reflect on Possibility...57

Attitude of Accountability 58

    Responsibility 59

    Empowerment 59

    Accountability..59

    Motivation..60

    Resilience...60

    Stories on Accountability 61

        Escalate Early and Often..61

        Following the Money 62

        In It to Win It 64

    Reflect on Accountability...66

Attitude of Gratitude...67

    Pass it On...69

    Grateful Service...71

        Grateful Customer Service...72

        Be a Grateful Server 75

        Be a Grateful Customer...76

    Stories on Gratitude..78

        Prove Them Wrong..78

        One Step at a Time...79

        Far Enough 83

    Reflect on Gratitude...86

Reflect on Attitude...87

2. Manage Your Goals 89

The Six P's..91

    Prepare...92

    Plan..94

    Perform..97

    Prevail..98

    Produce..99

    Perfect.. 101

Manage Your Resources 103

Stories on Goals 105

    Get Started 105

    How Hard Can it Be?.. 106

    Goal Setting Works... 108

Reflect on Goals 111

3. Invest in Yourself...113

Appearance Matters 114

Education and Training..115

Added Value Support...117

    Anticipate Needs... 118

    Ask Effective Questions.. 118

    Deliver On the Promise.. 122

    No Surprises.. 122

    How to Add Value.. 123

Elevator Pitch 124

Stories on Self-Investment..125

    Panic to Power.. 125

    Saving Lives 128

    An Extra Push 131

Reflect on Self-Investment..133

4. Live a Balanced Life 135

Balance With Self 136

    In All Areas... 137

    Self-Image.. 137

    Self-Compassion 138

Balance With Others...139

    Do the Right Thing 139

        The Golden Rule...140

        The Platinum Rule 140

    Resolve Conflict... 142

        When to Do Something.....................................143

        When to Do Nothing...146

Build Relationships.. 148
    Captain of the World..149
    P.L.U.T.O. Communication 150
    Politically Astute...151
    Value Diversity...153

Stories on Balance...154
    Always There...154
    Do the Right Thing..155
    Differences are Rewarding......................................157

Reflect on Balance..159

5. Embrace Change **161**

Anticipate Change..162

Acknowledge Change...162

Accept Change...163

Stories on Change 164
    Change Happens...164
    Change for Growth...166
    Life Lessons...168

Reflect on Change..171

6. S.M.I.L.E. Mentoring **173**

What is a Mentor? 173

How to Choose a Mentor..175

Who is Mentoring You?...179

Who are You Mentoring? 179

How to Be a Mentor..180

How to Be a Mentee..182

Stories on Mentoring...184
    Role Model and Mentor 184
    Go Figure...186
    I Matter...187
    My Mentors...191

Reflect on Mentoring...193

7. S.M.I.L.E. Continuously **195**

S.M.I.L.E. is Action 195

S.M.I.L.E. is Ageless 196

S.M.I.L.E. is Continuous..198

Reflect on S.M.I.L.E. 199

Appendix **201**

Goal Sheet Example 203

Status Report Example..204

Self-Management Tips...206

    Critical Thinking..206

    Organization 207

    Time Management 208

    Reflect on Self-Management...209

QR Code Index 210

Bibliography...**211**

Index... **215**

About the Author... **217**

ACKNOWLEDGMENTS

Thank you to **My People** who helped me set goals, supported me through setbacks, celebrated my successes, and made this book possible!

I would also like to thank Kathy Dreher, Ann Rizzardini, and Tiffany Strause for their valuable editorial reviews, and Nerissa Vance for a spectacular front cover design.

In addition, I am thankful to those who generously allowed me to share their stories: Catherine Vittorio, Stephen Davidson, Dr. Skip Hudson, Paul Bricker, Aggie Rucker, Fred Fernandez, Christopher McLaughlin, Shakeb "Shak" Kundiwala, Nick Cruz, Suzanne Thomas, John and Wilma Claussen, Caroline Claussen, Mark MacDonald, Nicole Aguilar, Kathy Dreher, Dianne Mount, Bruce Frericks, Rick Myers, and Alex Valladares.

My eternal gratitude goes to Fred Fernandez for his advice and counsel, detailed editorial reviews, passionate discussions, and above all, his friendship.

Finally, I am especially grateful for my strongest supporter and kindest critic, Kathy.

S.M.I.L.E. CHAPTERS		
1	S.	**Select Your Attitude**
2	M.	**Manage Your Goals**
3	I.	**Invest in Yourself**
4	L.	**Live a Balanced Life**
5	E.	**Embrace Change**
6		**S.M.I.L.E. Mentoring**
7		**S.M.I.L.E. Continuously**
8		
9		
10		
11		
12		

INTRODUCTION

Why This Book?

If you're like me, then you already have too much to read and remember. Wouldn't you prefer a summary of the key points in one book, versus trying to retain all the knowledge from many books? If yes, then this book is for you!

> *Knowledge is a process of piling up facts; wisdom lies in their simplification.*
>
> —*Martin H. Fischer*

You'll find this book to be concise and informative as well as useful and entertaining. First, I researched the vast knowledge of many experts and reduced it down to just their key points. I then organized it into an acronym that is easy to remember, "S.M.I.L.E." Next, I describe each letter in its own chapter: **S**elect Your Attitude, **M**anage Your Goals, **I**nvest in Yourself, **L**ive a Balanced Life, and **E**mbrace Change. Then I added a chapter on mentoring, and a chapter explaining how to use S.M.I.L.E. continuously throughout your life. Finally, I've included some interactive features that turn it into a handy reference guide. The result is a wealth of expert experience at your fingertips to help guide your own path to success.

> *Experience is the teacher of all things.*
>
> —*Julius Caesar*

People of most ages and backgrounds will understand the plain language used in this book. It's an easy read and has a layout in the form of a quick reference manual. You don't have to be a rocket scientist to understand it. I'm certainly not one, and I wrote it.

> *The finest language is mostly made up of simple unimposing words.*
>
> —*George Eliot*

Let's consider what's in the table of contents. You may have studied these topics before, or some of them may be new. In either case, I designed this book to read, research, and discuss the information with more experienced people. It's beneficial to learn from others who have already tried, failed, and then bounced back to achieve their goals. The result may be even greater success in life than you can imagine.

The only source of knowledge is experience.

—*Albert Einstein*

Many topics are brief, but this is by design. The objective is to reduce everything down to just the key points. Therefore, this book is most useful if you discuss it with other people, and then interpret the meaning and value for yourself.

Everyone in a complex system has a slightly different interpretation. The more interpretations we gather, the easier it becomes to gain a sense of the whole.

—*Margaret J. Wheatley*

This book in not intended for those people who have changed the world, they wrote it! You'll read quotations from some of the most insightful and successful figures in history. I think you'll find them to be interesting, thought provoking, and entertaining. Moreover, if their quotes help motivate you then so much the better!

The wisdom of the wise, and the experience of ages, may be preserved by quotation.

—*Isaac D'Israeli*

Do you like stories from people who have achieved great success? I do, but sometimes it's hard to relate to them. I appreciate their achievements, but I don't see myself making the same choices or following in their path. In this book, you'll read personal stories from people who are not famous nor have they changed the world. They are everyday people like you and me. They're successful because of the choices they made to become who they are today. They didn't fail by trying to become something they really didn't want to be.

To be yourself in a world that is constantly trying to make you something else is the greatest accomplishment.

—*Ralph Waldo Emerson*

You'll have many goals for success. It comes from accomplishing simple daily tasks, short-term objectives, and complex goals that take years to finish. You don't have to be the best at anything, nor change the world to be successful. Don't get overwhelmed by the achievement of others. You are the one who decides what success means to you!

> *Success is the doing, not the getting; in the trying, not the triumph. Success is a personal standard, reaching for the highest that is in us, becoming all that we can be. If we do our best, we are a success.*
>
> *—Zig Ziglar*

The guidance in this book will apply to most everyone, but there are exceptions. Some people are not mentally or physically able to make choices about their circumstances. Others come from a different culture or have a different philosophy. With that in mind, you'll read experiences from the lives of many different people. I hope they're engaging, insightful, and relatable to your own life.

> *Our Similarities bring us to a common ground; Our Differences allow us to be fascinated by each other.*
>
> *—Tom Robbins*

In summary, *S.M.I.L.E. for Success* is an interactive guide to help figure out what you want, how to get it, who "Your People" are, and why you need them. I consider it a privilege to present this information to you, and to future generations. If I'm able to help just one person get what they want, then I'll feel that I've achieved what this book is all about; success!

> *The greatest good you can do for another is not just to share your riches but to reveal to him his own.*
>
> *—Benjamin Disraeli*

Why This Design?

The global workforce is changing from the Baby Boomer to the Millennial Generation. According to studies by U.S. Bureau of Labor and Deloitte Consulting, Millennials will account for about one-third of the U.S. workforce in 2014 and 75% of the global workforce by 2025. The table below is a summary of generations and approximate age groups.

Generation Name	Approximate Birth Range	Age in 2025
Silent Generation	1925-1942	83-100
Baby Boomers	1943-1960	65-82
Busters or Gen X	1960-1980	45-65
Millennial or Gen Y	1980-2000	25-45
New Silent or Gen Z	2000-2014+	11-25

Each generation brings changes in how they learn. The Silent Generation learned from informal folklore and books in formal classrooms. Online technology has accelerated and expanded learning for later generations. The learning style of the Millennial Generation is the basis for the design of this book.

Millennials enjoy self-directed informal learning and eLearning, prefer speed and efficiency, and are comfortable with technology. They will require a transfer of knowledge from the experienced veterans of the current workforce. New programs for mentoring and eMentoring can pair veterans with Millennials. The veterans can share wisdom and organizational knowledge and conversely the Millennials can offer creativity and new ideas.

This book is an interactive guide to help knowledge transfer through mentoring. Its features include personal stories, reflective questions, note cards, and quick response (QR) codes.

- PERSONAL STORIES. Most of us enjoy reading stories from people who have changed the world, but some find it overwhelming to set such lofty goals for their own life. Instead, you'll read stories from people who are not famous nor changed the world. They're everyday people like you and me. Their stories are examples that success comes at different times in our lives, and sometimes in entertaining and unexpected ways.

- REFLECTIVE QUESTIONS. Each chapter ends with open-ended questions to reflect on and discuss with other people. It's important to stop and think about what you read. Not all the information will make sense, but there may be some words of wisdom you can use or pass on to another. A conversation with someone can make it clearer and each can decide if it's applicable to his or her own life. These questions are great for mentoring sessions to get a conversation started and to build the mentor-mentee relationship.

- NOTE CARDS. The note cards in each chapter will help retain the key points from the book. You may want to expand on them for personal visualization and affirmations. In addition, both mentors and mentees can use them during mentoring sessions.

- QR CODES. The appendix has a list of quick response (QR) code diagrams for each chapter in this book. To use a QR code, scan it with your smartphone app, and it will search the web for the topic coded in the diagram. Your browser will return web pages with links to various articles, books, and tips.

This book is not intended to be read in one sitting, cover to cover. Each chapter is worth spending time to reflect on. Some of the sections might be more relevant or timely to your situation, but I highly recommend going through them all. This book is intended to be discussed with *Your People*, and to facilitate knowledge sharing between generations.

All generations have something in common. It's the desire for success in our personal and professional lives as well as our relationships with family, friends, and co-workers. Whichever generation you're from, this book is a valuable resource for personal development and the development of others through mentoring.

Why Your People?

As mentioned before, this book is ideal for sharing and discussion with other people. If you just read it without discussing it, then you won't get much out of it. Learning from the experience of others will help achieve success faster and with fewer failures.

> *There is only one thing more painful than learning from experience, and that is not learning from experience.*
> —*Laurence J. Peter*

"Your People" are members of your family, friends, faith, mentors, workplace, or a professional resource such as an advisor, attorney, or physician. **Your People** are those who:

- Help define and manage goals.
- Give constructive feedback.
- Tell the truth in a caring manner even if it may hurt your feelings.
- Support you through setbacks.
- Celebrate success.

There are many people in your life, but only a few are truly one of **Your People**. Other people generally fit in one of the following categories:

- ACQUAINTANCE. Someone you know, but doesn't fit in any of the other categories.
- ENEMY. The opposite of **Your People**. You may choose to have a relationship or not.
- FRIEND. Someone you have a close relationship with, but may not be one of **Your People**.
- IMPOSTER. Pretends to be one of **Your People**, but you know better. You choose to continue the relationship or not.
- ROLE MODEL. A person you want to imitate their actions or behavior.
- STRANGER. A person you don't have a relationship with yet.

Only a few people have the experience and wisdom to be trusted with your success. Only you can determine who to be wary of, and who to give your confidence.

> *Be courteous to all, but intimate with few, and let those few*
> *be well tried before you give them your confidence.*
>
> —*George Washington*

It's normal to have a limited number of **Your People**. It may take some time and perseverance to find someone to trust with your future. However, financial, legal, medical, and personal issues are resolved better and faster by hiring a professional. Family and friends may not always have your best interest in mind, especially when it's needed the most. Choose **Your People** carefully.

> *Books, like friends, should be few and well chosen. Like*
> *friends, too, we should return to them again and again for,*
> *like true friends, they will never fail us—never cease to in-*
> *struct—never cloy.*
>
> —*Charles Caleb Colton*

Your People will give constructive feedback in a caring manner, even if it may hurt your feelings. Criticism is usually just pointing out the flaws or mistakes of others. For example, "You suck!" On the other hand, constructive feedback includes tips on how to improve. For example, "You'll do better next time with more practice."

> *True friends stab you in the front.*
>
> —*Oscar Wilde*

Read, research, and reflect on this book with **Your People**, then take action for success.

> *A truly good book teaches me better than to read it. I must*
> *soon lay it down, and commence living on its hint. What I*
> *began by reading, I must finish by acting.*
>
> —*Henry David Thoreau*

In short, you need **Your People** for help and support as you *S.M.I.L.E. for Success.* Let's get started together!

SELECT YOUR ATTITUDE	
1	**Attitude of Choice**
2	Everything you do is a choice and has consequences
3	**Attitude of Purpose**
4	Doer, Smiler, Solver, Victor
5	**Attitude of Possibility**
6	Possibility Blockers, Possibility Zone, Wizards
7	**Attitude of Accountability**
8	Responsible, Empowered, Accountable, Motivated
9	**Attitude of Gratitude**
10	Pass it On, Grateful Service; Server and Customer
11	
12	

1. SELECT YOUR ATTITUDE

Would you be surprised if I said you already know what it takes to be successful—and already have it? So what is it? It's the ability to "Select your Attitude!"

> *If you want to sum it up in a word, it is not difficult to do: success is, more than anything else and without a doubt, a question of attitude. What is your attitude?*
>
> —*Lou Tice*

ATTITUDE. The beliefs, values, and expectations we have about life determine our attitude. We can change our attitude by changing our beliefs and expectations. We don't have to change our core values, but we may adapt the way in which we use them in order to succeed in a changing world. The key points on attitude are:

- BELIEFS. Our beliefs are things we hold to be true, often without evidence or proof. What we hear or see from others, and what we are repeatedly exposed to (e.g. advertising) form beliefs. Our values stem from beliefs.

- VALUES. Our values are the beliefs we deem important or worthy. They include ethics (values about others), morals (values about ourselves), and norms (values about society). Our beliefs and values form expectations about others and ourselves.

- EXPECTATIONS. Our expectations are what we believe will happen in the future, whether realistic or not. According to sociologist Robert K. Merton, a self-fulfilling prophecy is either a true or a false prediction of the future.

> *I know not anything more pleasant, or more instructive, than to compare experience with expectation … it is by this kind of observation that we grow daily less liable to be disappointed.*
>
> —*Dr. Samuel Johnson*

ATTITUDE IS A CHOICE. Regardless of circumstances, you have a choice of attitude. You can choose a negative attitude, feel like a failure, and do nothing about it. Or, you can choose a positive attitude and feel like a success by doing something differently. Napoleon Hill and W. Clement Stone were among the greatest writers on success. In their landmark book, *Success Through a Positive Mental Attitude*, they lift up a positive mental attitude as the most essential of their seventeen principles for achieving success.

> *There is little difference in people, but that little difference makes a big difference! The little difference is attitude. The big difference is whether it is positive or negative.*
> —*Napoleon Hill and W. Clement Stone*

NEGATIVE ATTITUDE. A negative attitude is to believe that you're on your own, fate is predetermined, and nothing you can do will change the outcome.

> *Positive thinking will let you do everything better than negative thinking will.*
> —*Zig Ziglar*

POSITIVE ATTITUDE. A positive attitude is the belief that you can choose to do or become whatever you want. A positive mental attitude doesn't mean bad things won't happen. It means you can face a setback with the power to determine the outcome, versus feeling like a victim who is powerless to change the inevitable.

> *Nothing can stop the man with the right mental attitude from achieving his goal; nothing on earth can help the man with the wrong mental attitude.*
> —*Thomas Jefferson*

SELECT ALL ATTITUDES. Select all attitudes for success: Choice, Purpose, Possibility, Accountability, and Gratitude. Your attitude can help achieve even more than you thought to be possible!

> *Attitude, not Aptitude, determines Altitude.*
> —*Zig Ziglar*

ATTRACT POSITIVE RESULTS. Like most people, you probably don't want to be around someone with a negative attitude. You tend to be attracted to positive people. Two people cannot help but to achieve positive results together when they both have a positive attitude.

> *The person who sends out positive thoughts activates the world around him positively and draws back to himself positive results.*
>
> —*Norman Vincent Peale*

ATTITUDE IS CATCHING. One of the most renowned experts on success was the late Zig Ziglar. His groundbreaking book, *See You at the Top*, is an American classic. Zig emphasizes in his book that, "attitude is catching." In this chapter, I'll describe many attitudes that are worth catching. Your attitude will influence the attitudes of other people. The right mental attitude will inspire others and yourself to be the best that you can be.

> *The choice to have a great attitude is something that nobody or no circumstance can take from you.*
>
> —*Zig Ziglar*

ATTITUDE IS THE KEY. Don't just choose one attitude at a time. Choose as many as possible at the same time. Choose the right mental attitude, and choose success!

> *It is our attitude at the beginning of a difficult task which, more than anything else, will affect its successful outcome.*
>
> —*William James*

ATTITUDE AND BELIEF. The basic premise of *S.MI.L.E for Success* is that our attitude creates a self-fulfilling prophecy that says, "We become what we believe to be true."

> *You don't become what you want, you become what you believe.*
>
> —*Oprah Winfrey*

ATTITUDE OF CHOICE	
1	**Everything is a Choice**
2	There is nothing you "have to" do other than eventually die
3	You have the power to choose your own destiny
4	Use your power and choose to be happy
5	Every choice has a consequence; positive or negative
6	**Choose Your Response**
7	We cannot always choose what happens to us
8	We can always choose how to respond
9	Respond, don't react; stop, feel, think, act
10	There is a right time and right place to let emotions out
11	Take a time-out if necessary
12	

ATTITUDE OF CHOICE

When is the last time you had to make an important choice—one that could turn out good or bad? If it turns out very bad then it will heartlessly destroy both your confidence and life. At least that's how it seems at the time. Conversely, if it turns out good then a feeling of accomplishment will help your confidence soar. Everything we do in life is a choice. An "Attitude of Choice" is accepting responsibility for how we choose to act and behave.

> *I discovered I always have choices and sometimes it's only a choice of attitude.*
>
> —*Judith M. Knowlton*

Everything is a Choice

What do you really "have to" do in life? Think about it. You don't "have to" get an education, do fulfilling work, or be happy. There is literally nothing you "have to" do other than eventually die. Millions of people have heard this concept from the late Lou Tice, past Chairman and Co-founder of The Pacific Institute®. In his book, *A Better World, a Better You: The Proven Lou Tice "Investment in Excellence" Program*, Lou Tice explains that constructive motivation results from being accountable for our choices.

4

I learned from Lou that we have the ability to choose our own destiny, and happiness comes from accepting the accountability for our choices. I think about this every day and it serves me well. Always remember that you have the power to choose. Use your power and choose to be happy!

> *The wonders and beauty of life are all around you, right now, right where you are. All that is required is for you to be attentive and open to them and that you make a conscious choice to see and hear and experience them. So I ask you, do you choose to be happy today?*
>
> —*Lou Tice*

CONSEQUENCES. Choices have consequences. For example, if you don't pay creditors or taxes, there are negative consequences. On the other hand, there are positive consequences for managing your income and expenses. Only you can decide if choices are worth their consequences.

> *While we are free to choose our actions, we are not free to choose the consequences of our actions.*
>
> —*Stephen R. Covey*

Choose Your Response

We don't choose our parents or social and economic situation at birth. Furthermore, we don't choose to have unpreventable accidents. We cannot always choose what happens to us, but we can always choose how to respond.

> *The response to the challenges of life—purpose—is the healing balm that enables each of us to face up to adversity and strife.*
>
> —*Denis Waitley*

RESPOND, DON'T REACT. The reality of life is that sometimes things do not work out as expected. Reacting to a setback without thinking first can lead to embarrassing and regretful situations. It is perfectly okay to feel emotion about what happens. In fact, it's preferred. Getting feelings out can help let go of ill will that could negatively affect you or someone else later. The key is how you respond to the situation.

> *Life is ten percent what happens to you and ninety percent how you respond to it.*
>
> —*Lou Holtz*

STOP, FEEL, THINK, ACT. Do not immediately react to setbacks. Stop and deal with how you feel about what has happened. Then consider what the impact will be to others and yourself. Finally, choose an appropriate response relative to its impact.

> *If you don't like something change it; if you can't change it, change the way you think about it.*
>
> —*Mary Engelbreit*

RIGHT TIME AND PLACE. There is a right time and place to let out emotions. Some situations are appropriate to let them out in front of others. Other situations are not. You will learn to wait until it's the right time and place. Take a "time-out" if necessary and get away alone, or with **Your People**, to get feelings out and level your emotions.

> *Sometimes being a friend means mastering the art of timing. There is a time for silence. A time to let go and allow people to hurl themselves into their own destiny. And a time to prepare to pick up the pieces when it's all over.*
>
> —*Octavia Butler*

Stories on Choice

The following stories are on this section, *Attitude of Choice*:

- Tough Decisions
- Cause, Not Effect
- The Best

Tough Decisions

I know about tough decisions and choosing my responses. When I was in High School, my girlfriend and I had a child and I agreed to marry her. We were so young we couldn't get married in our State. Our parents had to drive us hundreds of miles to marry in another State. I assumed we would "grow up" together, but it didn't work out that way. We had a second child and grew even further apart over the next several years. Finally, I chose to end the marriage hoping it would give our children and us a better future.

My second marriage came years later. I fell in love with my girl-friend and her two young daughters during a long-distance romance that lasted several months. Yes, months. Apparently, I'm a slow learner. We married, I adopted the girls, and we were a loving family until they became teenagers. Our disagreement on parenting issues reached an impasse. The situation broke the family bond and our marriage.

No one forced me into these situations; I made these choices all by myself. Not all my choices have been good ones, but I've been accountable for all of them. I sought out self-help books, courses, and counselors for myself. I was an active participant in marriage counseling with my wives and children. I never missed an alimony or child support payment. In retrospect, I accepted accountability for my choices and I took pride in providing for my family, even when we were no longer together.

I could've felt sorry for myself all these years, but instead I choose to be thankful because I learned to make better choices. Now I have a wonderful marriage with my third wife. I know what you're thinking. Yes, it's my **third** marriage—and last—according to my loving wife. We have two adult children, two adopted adult children, two adult stepchildren, and four beautiful grandchildren. That's a lot of tough decisions, and wonderful life experiences. I will always be accountable for the past and optimistic about the future.

My story is an example of how bad choices can result in a negative situation, and how good choices can turn a negative situation into a positive life experience. You may not have been recovering from bad choices as long as I have, but you have an opportunity that I didn't have earlier in my life. You can select an Attitude of Choice now, and use it to make positive choices for the rest of your life!

Our lives are a sum total of the choices we have made.
— *Wayne Dyer*

Cause, Not Effect

Catherine is a professional educator that holds a Multiple Subject Credential and an Administrative Credential, who lives with her second husband, her best friend. Together they have five adult children. They love family time and look forward to planning outdoor vacations enjoying the sanctity of nature. Catherine enjoys reading non-fiction, reflective writing, quilting, and organizing her church in serving the homeless at a local church shelter. She navigates through life by embracing change and setting goals. Here is her story.

"As an inner city child of poverty, I knew I wanted to make a difference in the lives of others at a relatively young age. After High School, I attended college and earned a Bachelor of Science in Child Psychology. I worked as a Psych Technician at a private firm setting playtime scenarios to help children express their feelings and emotions. When I saw hurting kids, it saddened me; I didn't want them to hurt anymore. I knew they needed a pathway to learn to become good adults and to think and ask questions for themselves. I decided to make a change to help children before they needed therapy. I wanted to change the cause rather than have to treat the effect of their troubles.

After graduation, I worked at a small child development center, held various positions, eventually met my first husband, and continued my education. There were several times over the thirteen years that I was able to transfer as we moved our family to adapt with our changing careers.

After one particular move, we settled into a new church that was expanding its after-hours childcare program into a private school. The Pastor approached me to start the school and I did. I enjoyed being able to impact children's lives socially, emotional as well as spiritually.

In addition, I felt an inner passion for teaching growing inside. Developing the whole child brought me much joy. I wanted to be the cause rather than try to correct the effect of their development.

As the economy became more strained, the church private school attendance began to decline and my contract was in jeopardy. I set a goal to earn my Master's Degree in Education, which would increase my marketability in the public school system. As anticipated, the following year my contract was not renewed. At a time when jobs in education were limited, my preparation paid off and I was hired immediately upon applying in a local district.

After many years of teaching, I came to realize that my real passion is teaching teachers. I continued to set goals and have since completed a Masters in Administration and Educational Leadership (MAE). I enjoy being the cause of a child's education rather than the effect of poor teaching.

I'm a very goal driven person and I'm big on Ghandi, "Be the change you want to see in the world." How I navigate through my life is to set the end goal, then map it out backwards. Being in each place, I am involved and informed; serving, learning, and navigating. I like to be the cause, not the effect!

Speaking of goals, after a recent milestone birthday I wanted to do something huge. My husband thought I was a bit nutty for wanting to try skydiving! I set a goal to get in shape a few months before the jump. I achieved my goal and experienced one of the most exhilarating experiences of my life. I love my husband even more for getting outside his comfort zone and jumping with me!

Speaking of change, I had a pivotal time in my life several years ago. My mom was diagnosed with cancer and died only three weeks later. Then my husband of twenty years asked for a divorce. At the same time, my contract wasn't renewed at the church school. Over a period of six months, I experienced every big life change except dying myself. Everything was gone (except my beautiful children). Faith got me thorough and helped me make it a year of re-creation instead of total despair.

9

I grew to know myself better because I was by myself. I kept on navigating; I learned to be a single mother, raised two children, and eventually married again. Nothing that happened around me changed who I was. I believe in being the cause of who I am, not the effect. The death of my mother, a divorce, and the loss of a job wasn't going to make me a victim. I wasn't going to be an effect of my ex-husband's choice. I wasn't going to be an effect of the choices made by the board of directors of the private school. I am the cause, not the effect of whom I am and who I will become!"

Be the cause, not the effect of your destiny.

—*Catherine Vittorio*

The Best

Stephen is a medical lab technician serving in the U.S. Army. He enjoys physical fitness, sports, movies, and activities with friends and family. Stephen has always wanted to be the best at everything, but he's learned some lessons about choices along the way. Here is his story, as told by his mother.

"Stephen wanted to be great at an early age. He was never satisfied with being 'just okay.' He was in the top one percent of students in elementary school. He excelled in High School where every teacher knew his name. He was a good-looking boy and all the girls wanted to be with him. I love my son to death, but he needs to be the best and anything less upsets him.

Basketball was a passion for Stephen. He always had a ball with him dribbling everywhere we went. Most kids make the team in their sophomore year of High School. He was too busy with schoolwork that year, so he worked hard to make the team when he was a junior. The coach looked down on Stephen because the coach felt he didn't put in the time to earn his spot on the team. Stephen became discouraged and wanted to quit but his father and I wouldn't let him. He had to learn that he wouldn't always be the best, and people wouldn't always treat him fairly. He wasn't a superstar, so over time his interest changed to other sports. He learned that what you love is not always what you were meant to do.

After High School, Stephen chose a well-known college with a renowned Engineering program. Actually, the pretty girls at the open house may have influenced his decision. Nevertheless, I was proud of my son! Stephen absolutely loved Engineering! He loved the challenge of learning and being in the Honors program. Unfortunately, starting in his second year, he wasn't able to get the courses he wanted. He had to take other classes where the professors were unmotivated and in turn, Stephen lost focus in their classes.

Stephen has the need to be the best. He's going to be "Stephen Somebody", don't they know? Everything had always come easily to him; he shouldn't have to work so hard to get it! While his interest faded, his partying increased and his grades suffered.

Stephen was barely passing at this point. The college was full of high achievers. His classmates would get a 95% on their paper and worry it wasn't good enough. They weren't interested in study groups that could help Stephen get back on track. His friendships reverted to his friends in High School. They are all fine young men, but none aspired to go to college or have professional careers. His need to be the best had determined his peer group.

Work replaced college and his need to be the best continued. He made "all-star" of the year within six months at his job at a retail-clothing store. Within a year, he became the assistant manager. He made good money but, living at home, he didn't have any expenses. He figured he would be the boss someday so why go back to school. Then, of course, a shady car dealer sold Stephen a shiny new sports car. He couldn't afford it, but he looked good driving a car that was the best; just like him.

The retail job started to frustrate Stephen. New managers came and went, and none took the time to know him or care about his future. Finally, one manager told Stephen to leave his job because he was far more qualified than what he was doing. For this reason, the manager refused to promote Stephen. It was probably the best thing that could happen—someone other than his family who truly believed in him! Eventually his frustration peaked and he quit. Unfortunately, another job was hard to find.

My heart sank as I saw my son in debt, no job, and no scholarship. His options were dwindling but fortunately, he took the military aptitude and placement tests. He scored so high that the Army offered him training to become an electronic technician. Things were looking up and I was encouraged my son was on his way to be the best!

Stephen was in great shape so he had no problem completing basic training with awards in physical fitness and marksmanship. He graduated in the top three of his class in technical school and earned the opportunity to complete his training in Hawaii. He excelled in school, made rank, and then on to another assignment in Georgia. The Army mistakenly identified Stephen as a field medic and assigned him to a combat unit preparing to go to war in Afghanistan. I was terrified! The last thing I wanted was for my son to experience combat when that wasn't what he signed up to do.

The Army reclassified Stephen as a lab tech, he excelled at his job, found several opportunities for growth, received his Bachelor's degree, and was promoted to Sargent. He has a promising future regardless if he continues his military service or re-enters the civilian workforce.

My son has learned that choices don't always work out. He admits that he gets frustrated, but he knows he must make the next best choice instead of succumbing to his disappointment. I am very proud of my son and love him endlessly. I support his choices and I only want the best for him. I am confident that he will overcome all obstacles and become the best he can be!"

> *You better be good to me because I may be your boss someday.*
>
> —*Stephen Davidson*

Reflect on Choice

Reflect on the following and discuss with *Your People:*

1. What is an Attitude of Choice?
2. What things in life do I absolutely have to do, and have no choice not to?
3. What choices have I made recently that turned out to have negative consequences?
4. Which turned out to have positive consequences?
5. When have I reacted instead of responded (stop, feel, think, act)?
6. Describe a situation where I was able to "respond, not react" and how did it make me feel?
7. Do I think about the right time and place before I respond?
8. What do I do when I have to make a decision and there is no time to think about it?
9. How have I used an Attitude of Choice to help me with my goals?
10. What opportunities do I have in the near future to select an Attitude of Choice?

ATTITUDE OF PURPOSE	
1	**Doer**
2	Be a Doer; not dabbler, dreamer, talker, or wisher
3	Focus brings clarity; avoid distractions to become your best
4	**Smiler**
5	A smile makes a good impression and is contagious
6	A smile can reduce stress, build morale, and improve results
7	**Solver**
8	Bring solutions, not problems
9	Focus on solving the problem, not who to blame
10	**Victor**
11	A victim feels powerless to change what happens to them
12	A victor is responsible for choices and accountable for results

ATTITUDE OF PURPOSE

There are several attitudes described in this chapter. So what do you do with all these attitudes? Use them to achieve your purpose in life! In the book, *The Success Principles: How to Get From Where You Are to Where You Want to Be*, bestselling author and success expert Jack Canfield writes that once you understand what brings the greatest joy, then you'll have an insight into your purpose. Do you know what your purpose is?

> *If you can tune into your purpose and really align with it, setting goals so that your vision is an expression of that purpose, then life flows much more easily.*
>
> —Jack Canfield

IT DEFINES YOU. An "Attitude of Purpose" is what defines, fulfills, and makes you happy. It's what you want out of life and what legacy you want to leave behind.

> *If you're alive, there's a purpose for your life.*
>
> —Rick Warren

IT'S YOUR PASSION. Your purpose is a passion to get what you want, and the motivation for success.

> *If you can't figure out your purpose, figure out your passion. Your passion will lead you right into your purpose.*
>
> —*Bishop T.D. Jakes*

ASK WHY. Why do you want to be successful? Is it for accomplishment, challenge, meaning, relationships, wealth, or something else?

> *Being the richest man in the cemetery doesn't matter to me. Going to bed at night saying we've done something wonderful, that's what matters to me.*
>
> —*Steve Jobs*

ASK WHAT. What are the results you want from success? Is it happiness, joy, peace, satisfaction, or something else?

> *Success is getting what you want; happiness is wanting what you get.*
>
> —*Ingrid Bergman*

IF YOU DON'T KNOW. If you don't know what you do want, then move away from what you don't want.

> *The path to our destination is not always a straight one. We go down the wrong road, we get lost, we turn back. Maybe it doesn't matter which road we embark on. Maybe what matters is that we embark.*
>
> —*Barbara Hall*

WISH VS. WANT. The difference between wishing and wanting for something is taking action to get it.

> *Stop the mindless wishing that things would be different. Rather than wasting time and emotional and spiritual energy in explaining why we don't have what we want, we can start to pursue other ways to get it.*
>
> —*Greg Anderson*

GET WHAT YOU WANT. If you're stuck and don't know what your purpose is, then involve **Your People** to help figure it out. If you know what you want, then choose an Attitude of Purpose to get it!

> *You can have everything in life you want, if you will just help other people get what they want.*
>
> *— Zig Ziglar*

Doer

Most great ideas and accomplishments started with just a dream. A world without dreamers would be dull and uninspiring. The difference between the dreamer and the "Doer" is **action**. Two people can have the same skills and desires, but have very different outcomes. Why? One acted and the other did not.

> *Work gives you meaning and purpose and life is empty without it.*
>
> *— Stephen Hawking*

DOERS DO IT. Some people dabble, dream, talk, or wish about doing something. Other people are Doers and get it done. You may be nodding your head because you know exactly what I'm saying. You probably know some of the following types of people:

- DABBLERS are always doing something, but are quickly bored or frustrated and move on to something else.
- DREAMERS have big ideas, but get distracted chasing the next big one.
- TALKERS love to tell you all about what they are "gonna" do, but never do it.
- WISHERS have a longing for something, but don't do what it takes to obtain it.

PARALYSIS BY ANALYSIS. In addition, some people may have a fear of failure or wait until everything is perfect. This "paralysis by analysis" causes them to lose focus on setting and achieving their goals. Doers are what Pareto calls the vital few, also known as the 80-20 rule. It says that 80% of results come from 20% of the people who try. Doers are the 20%!

> *One reason so few of us achieve what we truly want is that we never direct our focus; we never concentrate our power. Most people dabble their way through life, never deciding to master anything in particular.*
>
> —*Tony Robbins*

AVOID DISTRACTIONS. Many of us have something in common with championship athletes. We have a strong motivation to achieve goals, and the will to prevail over setbacks. However, athletes have the ability to avoid distractions and concentrate all of their attention on what they are doing. That's what makes them the best in their sport. We have the possibility to be champions: avoid distractions, focus on what we are doing, and achieve goals to become the best that we can be.

> *Work is hard. Distractions are plentiful. And time is short.*
>
> —*Adam Hochschild*

FOCUS BRINGS CLARITY. In photography, focusing the camera lens brings clarity to a visual image. The same is true for goals. Focus brings clarity to what you want, and helps to achieve goals by avoiding distractions.

> *Truth and clarity are complementary.*
>
> —*Niels Henrik David Bohr*

MULTI-TASKING. We all do it: texting while walking, using social media during meetings, and looking at smartphones instead of each other at dinner. In his article *Multitasking, social media and distraction: Research review*, Wihbey lists several recent studies on distraction that show it's much less efficient than people believe. Multitasking is very useful at times, but it can make us susceptible to error or even harmful to our health.

> Since distraction is the opposite of focus, your ability to focus is directly related to how well you are able to consistently avoid and eliminate distractions.
>
> —Tony Jeary

BE A DOER. If you're a dreamer and want to become a Doer, then start by avoiding distractions and focus on goals. You can S.M.I.L.E. to bring clarity to goals, and then use them to achieve the purpose for your life. Be the 20%. Be a Doer!

> I know that I have the ability to achieve the object of my Definite Purpose in life, therefore, I DEMAND of myself persistent, continuous action toward its attainment, and I here and now promise to render such action.
>
> —Napoleon Hill

Smiler

Have you noticed when you smile at people, they'll usually smile back? It's effortless and natural to use a smile to communicate kindness, approval, or amusement. Most people will perceive a positive attitude just from the smile on your face.

If you turn the book over you'll see my "mug shot." You cannot imagine how difficult it was for me to sit for this photo—or maybe you can! I don't have a movie star smile so I had to practice in front of the mirror. Then it took way-too-many shots to get one that I liked. Thank goodness for digital cameras!

I was in disbelief at how some of the pictures came out. I just knew I had the biggest smile possible because my cheeks were hurting, but when I checked, it wasn't so. In my frustration to get it right, I wasn't in the mood to smile. I had to force a smile on my face to get the shot I needed. Then, something happened. I felt much better!

Am I really suggesting that you do the same? Yes, I am! Practice in the mirror, take as many pictures as necessary, show them to **Your People,** and get their opinion.

You might want to upload a photo to online profiles at work and on social media. I'm sure you'll end up with a smile that will make a great first impression—and you'll feel good about it!

> *A warm smile is the universal language of kindness.*
> —*William Arthur Ward*

A SMILE IS CONTAGIOUS. Sometimes you just won't feel like it. Even when you're angry, ill, or sad, remember to smile at others. You want them to know it's not their fault and you still care about them. In turn, they will appreciate your positive attitude. Do this at work, social events, and especially at home among your loved ones. A smile is contagious and promotes goodwill to others, as well as a favorable impression of the one wearing it. And it makes you feel better doing it. Smile, and be contagious!

> *Nothing is so contagious as example; and we never do any great good or evil which does not produce its like.*
> —*Francois de La Rochefoucauld*

SMILE FOR SUCCESS. It was inevitable, so here it is—the literal interpretation of S.M.I.L.E. as in the smile on your face. Well, why not? Many studies show that a smile and a good sense of humor is one of the keys to success. Companies such as Southwest Airlines in the United States and kulula.com in South Africa use it to build their brand. Their positive fun culture attracts and retains both customers and employees, and makes them smile!

> *A smile is the light in your window that tells others that there is a caring, sharing person inside.*
> —*Denis Waitley*

HUMOR IS WELCOME. It's easy to smile when having a good time. Tasteful humor that's appropriate to the situation is always welcome. People enjoy having fun, but you may have to tone it down at times. Humor tends to have an edge to it, so choose humor that is appropriate to the situation.

> *Humor is the good natured side of a truth.*
> —*Mark Twain*

HUMOR IS HUMANIZING. The ability to laugh at others and ourselves is what makes us human. It can reduce stress, stimulate creative thinking, build trust, improve morale, and increase productivity. It's a win-win for everyone!

> *A sense of humor... is needed armor. Joy in one's heart and some laughter on one's lips is a sign that the person down deep has a pretty good grasp of life.*
>
> —*Hugh Sidey*

Solver

Problems are part of everyday life at home and work. No matter how experienced people are, and how good a process is, things will go wrong. When a problem occurs, people tend to react by avoiding it, making a snap decision, or blaming others. Avoiders think the problem will go away by itself, but it usually gets worse. Snappers just react without thinking through the solution or its impact. Often they don't even understand what the problem is in the first place. Blamers don't have accountability so they try to save face by absolving themselves of any wrongdoing, and deflect it to others.

In contrast, Solvers are fixers. They use a methodical approach to focus on how to fix the problem versus who to blame. When something goes wrong, be patient and don't jump to unfounded conclusions. Choosing your response can avoid an embarrassment at home or a "career limiting move" at work.

> *People mistakenly assume that their thinking is done by their head; it is actually done by the heart which first dictates the conclusion, then commands the head to provide the reasoning that will defend it.*
>
> —*Anthony de Mello*

SOLUTIONS, NOT PROBLEMS. When you report a problem, what do you expect the boss to do? Sometimes it's a quick fix, other times it cannot be resolved. Most of the time, it's not going to get resolved on the spot. You'll probably be asked for a recommendation, or assigned to a team to resolve the problem. More often than not, you're going to be involved in the resolution, so why not bring solutions instead of problems.

You bring solutions by defining the problem and offering a plan for resolution. Take some time to think about the problem and its impact, and a couple of options on how to resolve it; plan "A" and plan "B". It's best to write down what the problem is in one or two concise sentences. Then schedule an appropriate time and place to present a solution. Define the problem, describe its impact, and make recommendations to resolve it. Your boss may come up with other options you didn't think of, or didn't know about.

The boss will prioritize the problem against all the others. Depending on where your issue lands in the priority queue, you'll know how much focus and resources the organization will expend to resolve it. If you present facts to explain why the problem has a greater impact, or can result in greater benefit, then you'll have a better chance of getting it moved up in the queue. You'll also have a better chance of gaining respect and advancement opportunities in the organization.

If the problem doesn't get resolved, don't just complain about it. Instead, come up with a work-around. The problem is not fixed, but it may be easier to tolerate. Instead of just complaining, even the smallest work-around will bring positive results. Bring solutions, not problems—you'll be glad you did!

> *If you took one-tenth the energy you put into complaining and applied it to solving the problem, you'd be surprised by how well things can work out.*
>
> —*Randy Pausch*

DON'T COMPLAIN. Complaining won't fix the problem. It just creates a new one by poisoning the organization with a negative attitude. A positive attitude attracts advancement opportunities. A negative one attracts the opposite. Be a solver, not a complainer!

> *Complaining does not work as a strategy. We all have finite time and energy.*
>
> —*Randy Pausch*

DON'T WHINE. Complaining may temporarily make you feel better, but when nothing changes, you'll feel even worse—and so will others around you.

> *Any time we spend whining is unlikely to help us achieve our goals. And it won't make us happier.*
>
> —*Randy Pausch*

SOLVERS CARE. Would you rather be on a team of solvers or complainers? The answer may be obvious, but it's important and therefore worth consideration. How the boss perceives you will influence how you're treated. Perception can lead to success or failure. However, be careful at home. Loved ones don't always want their problems solved. Sometimes they just want you to listen and show you care. They need you to be a "care-er", not a "solve-er."

> *Nobody cares how much you know, until they know how much you care.*
>
> —*Theodore Roosevelt*

KEY POINTS. One way to solve problems is by using the "Six P's" method. There is more detail on it in the chapter *Manage Your Goals*. The method consists of action verbs: to prepare, to plan, to perform, to prevail, to produce, and to perfect. The key points of solving problems are to:

- PREPARE. Identify the problem and its impact. Write down a concise problem definition in one or two sentences. If the impact is very low, then it may not be worth addressing. If the impact is very high, then it may be a "world hunger" issue that cannot be fixed. If the problem has sufficient impact and is resolvable, then people will want to help find a solution.

- PLAN. Use brainstorming and risk planning methods for problem resolution.

    - BRAINSTORMING. Assemble the team and brainstorm options for resolving the problem. Allow everyone to present ideas no matter how silly or improbable. Even if an option is impossible, it may inspire others to think of new ideas. It's imperative not to evaluate anything yet. Don't allow anyone to say, "That'll never work." Do allow "what if?" and appropriate humor to stimulate creativity and innovation. Next, evaluate all the ideas. Pick the ideas apart and determine which are best. Then decide on the most viable options. Finally, prioritize the list based on the impact and resources needed (time, money, and people).

- RISK PLANNING. Determine the best course of action, including backup plans. Typically, the best course of action is to resolve the highest impact problem first, using the fewest resources. Identify risks and a plan on how to accept, transfer, or mitigate them.

- PERFORM. Get acceptance, line up resources, and then execute the plan.

- PREVAIL. Focus on solving the problem, not who to blame. How the problem occurred is more important than who did it. How to resolve it is even more important. For example, when a process fails, people will be more open to identifying the cause if they know they won't be blamed for just doing their job.

- PRODUCE. Everyone involved in the plan is a stakeholder. Stakeholders are accountable to implement the plan. The leader is accountable to keep all stakeholders updated with progress; from start, to finish, to follow-up with lessons learned. Solve the problem and celebrate success with all stakeholders.

- PERFECT. Assemble the team, look back at what happened, and brainstorm how things can be better the next time.

Victor

We all know who the victims are. When something goes wrong, they're the first to say, "It's not my fault, they did it to me!" Victims may be able to get by in life, but it would be difficult for them to be successful. Victims don't acknowledge responsibility for their actions. They blame outside forces for their circumstances.

If it's never our fault, we can't take responsibility for it. If we can't take responsibility for it, we'll always be its victim.
—Richard Bach

VICTIMS. Victims feel powerless to change what happens in life. People are not born with a victim mentality—they develop this habit over time. Like any habit, it's possible to change a victim mentality. However, a habit can be very difficult to change on your own. Involve **Your People** if necessary to help change bad habits.

> *It is easier to prevent bad habits than to break them.*
>
> *—Benjamin Franklin*

VICTORS. In contrast, "Victors" know what they want out of life and are willing to take risks to get it. Victors own the responsibility for their choices whether successful or not. Successful people are Victors. They are accountable for their mistakes, learn from them, and then try again using a different approach.

> *Be a victor, not a victim.*
>
> *—Joel Osteen*

BE ACCOUNTABLE. Just as attitude is the key to success, accountability is the key to being a Victor. Accept the rewards when choices succeed, or accept the consequences when they don't.

> *The best years of your life are the ones in which you decide your problems are your own. You do not blame them on your mother, the ecology, or the president. You realize that you control your own destiny.*
>
> *—Albert Ellis*

BE A VICTOR. Victims have all of the S.M.I.L.E. resources available to help themselves transform into Victors. Victims feel disempowered because they believe that destiny is predetermined, and most things happen by chance. On the other hand, Victors believe that most things happen by choice. Their attitude creates a self-fulfilling prophecy: we become what we believe to be true. Clearly, accountability is pivotal for becoming successful. S.M.I.L.E. and with the support of **Your People**, you too can become a Victor!

> *Your beliefs become your thoughts, Your thoughts become your words, Your words become your actions, Your actions become your habits, Your habits become your values, Your values become your destiny.*
>
> *—Mahatma Gandhi*

Stories on Purpose

The following stories are on this section, *Attitude of Purpose*:

- One Purpose
- Many Purposes
- Problem Architect
- Problem Solved

One Purpose

Arthur "Skip" Hudson, DDS, MS, agreed to share a personal story about his one purpose. He decided what it was early in life and it has been his passion to this day. Here is his story.

He knew what he wanted to be since the age of sixteen. The oldest son of five children, Skip was very popular in High School. He was good-looking, charismatic, and played on the football team. He dated an attractive cheerleader, conceived a child, and was marred while still in school. He worked odd jobs and eventually started working for his father. Skip's father started the family Orthodontic practice in 1929. Skip helped with the lab work and learned how to make and adjust orthodontic appliances from his father. Skip knew he wanted to follow in his father's footsteps. His passion increased, and soon it became his purpose.

After completing his Associates of Science degree from a community college, Skip was accepted to the University of Southern California (USC) to pursue his purpose. He had a young and growing family to support so he had to work while in college. Seven years later, he graduated from his Dentistry and Ortho programs then joined the family business. Skip shared the practice for a dozen years before his father passed away. Skip continued to grow the family practice and fulfill his purpose

His marriage ended, eventually remarried, and his family grew to seven children. The practice grew to a staff of sixteen, and Skip became the most popular Orthodontist in the area. He treats patients from ages 3 to 80 because "It's never too late to have a beautiful smile!" His clientele includes famous movie stars, entertainers, and he provides free treatment for low-income families.

His staff shares Skip's passion for his work. Most have been with him for over twenty years. The daily staff meeting includes a round table with everyone sharing a positive thought for the day. Whether it's an office prank to stick a balloon to his back undetected, or involving the patients in a race to see who can remove appliances the fastest, Skip has truly nurtured a family practice. Repeat patients feel like they belong to the family, and he is regarded as "everybody's dad."

Work/life balance has always been important to Skip. He takes care of himself so he can lead his staff and serve his patients. He is a road cyclist, has run in the New York City marathon, and loves boating. He enjoys time with his family and grandchildren and is active in their lives.

When Dr. Skip is asked when he will retire, he joyfully answers, "What, and stop doing what I love?" Whenever that time comes, everyone will remember their "dad" fondly. Dr. Skip shows his passion with his infectious smile, charismatic personality, and his service to family, patients, and staff. His one purpose.

Flexibility is the hallmark of good health.

— Dr. Skip Hudson

Many Purposes

Many people know exactly what their purpose is. I can't tell you how many people I've met over the years with that one burning passion for what they like to do. They build their entire lives around it: art, career, exercise, music, sports, volunteering, you name it. They know their one true purpose in life and I truly admire them. However, I am not one of them.

It was the last year in high school when my parents gave me the news; I had to leave the family home the day I turned 18. Maybe I'm exaggerating; I think I had until the day after. At least that's what I believed so it must be true. Anyway, I had absolutely no idea what I was going to do, nor did I have a particular passion for anything other than girls, but that's a different story.

I will always remember the day I was in chemistry class and a summons came from the principal's office. My Army recruiter was there with another official-looking military guy. They both were in their full dress uniform with spit-shined shoes, medals, and stripes all the way down their sleeves. Wow, was I impressed! The principal closed all the blinds, invited me to sit down, then excused himself and quietly closed the door behind him. The official looking one leaned over the desk and, in a very low and secretive voice said, "Son, your Country needs you!" Hook in mouth. I asked, "What will I be doing?" He looked at my recruiter, then turned back to me and quietly said, "Its top secret and we cannot tell you here." Hook sunk in mouth. "Will I get a guaranteed contract?" I heard "Absolutely!", then the line pulled tight and they reeled me into the boat!

I enlisted in the Army Security Agency as an "electronic warfare technician." I could tell you about it but, well, you know the rest. I recovered from basic training, then off to electronics school. I discovered my passion and decided I was going to be a television technician. After my service in the Army, I could see myself proudly working at my own bench in the back of a retail store—a real "bench tech." Purpose #1.

Soon I learned that if I graduated at the top of my class then I would get a promotion (translated more money), and my choice of duty assignment. I did so, and I got the promotion. My choice of duty assignments were Korea by myself, or stay with my family as an instructor of basic electronics. Oh, by the way, my family could move out of a rat-infested apartment to a beautiful home on the Army base.

You guessed it! I got my lab coat and chalk holder (I realize some of you have no idea what chalk is or why it requires a holder), and completed instructor training. They paired me with the best educator I've ever known, who became my mentor. The very first day on the lectern, I discovered I had a knack for conveying knowledge. The faces of my students would light up when they finally understood some random theory I was diagramming all over the chalkboard. I fell in love with teaching. Purpose #2.

After four memorable years, my employer offered me yet another choice. Korea again by myself, reenlist and take my family with me to Germany, or leave the Army for that television repair job. My mentor helped me realize that I had a substantial mastery of electronics theory, but no practical experience. Nobody would likely hire me. I chose to reenlist and enjoy the adventure of living outside the United States while gaining the experience I need to be a successful bench tech.

We arrived in Berlin and discovered a fascinating city, new friends, and a love of beer. Oh, and apple schnapps. Moving on, I gained a ton of practical experience in the Army. I fixed electronic equipment and learned about this new thing called a computer. After rising to one of the top technicians, they recruited me to work "undercover." I received the Army Commendation medal for something very cool I did but cannot disclose. The Army was good for me, but it wasn't my passion so at the end of my duty I accepted an honorable discharge.

I came back to the U.S. to look for a bench tech job but found a shocking surprise instead. My dream job that paid a substantial wage before I left now paid about the same as I made in the Army. Apparently, everyone wanted to be a bench tech and all the trade schools helped to flood the market. The job pool surged and wages plummeted. I looked around and finally settled for a low-paying job fixing computers at a NASA tracking station in the middle of nowhere. Again, this wasn't my passion.

Living there turned out to be advantageous for me. Digital Equipment Corporation (DIGITAL) just installed one of their largest computers at the Army base nearby, and needed someone to keep it working. I aced the interview and they hired me. On my first day, my new boss flew me in her small plane to work and handed me the keys to my first company car. Sweet! Then it was off to school to learn how to fix this newfangled machine and start my new career.

At the time, computers were mysterious and this monstrosity was one-of-a-kind. The customer welcomed me as if I was a hero who arrived to save the day! Soon thereafter, the thing stopped working—it "crashed." It literally took every skill I learned in my life to get it back up and running: electronics, teaching, computers, deep breathing, and maybe a little luck. Well, I did it and I was the "rock star" of the day. Yes, I found it. Purpose #3.

Fast-forwarding now, one of my mentors guided me to become a senior technician, manager, operations manager, and on a fast track to become a vice president. This was still not my purpose. Then I got "the call" from another mentor offering me a project management job. You see, at the time you became a "project manager" if you couldn't do anything else. People saw it as having "one foot out the door." Fortunately, I had my finger on the pulse of the IT industry and I understood that a new profession was emerging, and so did my mentor. Ta-da! Project Management.

I accepted the job and soon achieved the coveted Project Management Professional (PMP®) certification. DIGITAL became Compaq through a corporate acquisition and they needed someone to help their services sales reps translate customer problems into solutions. There wasn't a position for this yet, but I took the leap and tried it. To my surprise I was good at it and, with my finger still on the pulse, realized that yet another profession was emerging called a "Solution Architect."

Meanwhile, I took night and online classes and earned an Associate of Science in Electronics Technology, a Bachelor of Science in Business, and a Master of Science in Project Management. As it turns out, I was preparing myself for this new profession all along and didn't realize it!

As a Solution Architect, I collaborate with customers to understand their business and technical requirements. Then I design a customized service solution that will meet or exceed their requirements and is profitable to the company. Over time, Compaq became Hewlett-Packard, my title changed to "Business Consultant", and I found a challenging job that demands all the skills I've learned throughout my life. Purpose #4.

As you can see, I've had several "purposes" in my past, and probably more to come in the future. I often did well at "selecting my attitude", although *My People* had to work overtime to help me now and again. I'm proud of myself the way I "managed my goals." I definitely "invested in myself", but I haven't always been able to "live a balanced life." I feel I'm pretty darn good at "embracing change." I am eternally grateful to my mentors who believed in me, supported me, kicked my ass, and opened doors for me along the way. For anyone surprised by the words "kicked my ass", it's a technical term for "constructive feedback."

Ask **Your People** about their "purpose". You may find that, like me, they too had an interesting journey to get where they are. I know you'll have an adventurous journey to find your own "purpose", even if you aren't sure what it is today. Enjoy your journey!

Problem Architect

I work in the services division of a large computer company as a Solution Architect. As the title suggests, my job is to find solutions to problems. An important part of the job is to collaborate with the delivery team who has to implement the solution, and together we create a risk management plan. We identify what risks are in the solution, and document a plan of how to accept, transfer, or mitigate them.

Occasionally, we get an unwelcome member on the team. It's the dreaded "Problem Architect." Anything that could possibly, and impossibly, go wrong, will! The epitome of a Problem Architect is one who holds the team hostage for 45-minutes. They go on and on insisting that a one thousand dollar risk could tank the multi-million dollar solution. The resolution is obvious to everyone but them. The risk is literally a "rounding error" in the profitability of the solution. In other words, the right thing to do is just accept the extremely low impact risk. Then move on so we don't miss an important and costly risk elsewhere.

Find solutions to problems instead of complaining about them. Focus on the solution so you won't miss potential problems by being distracted. Be a Solver, as in a Solution Architect, not a Problem Architect!

Problem Solved

Nothing irritates me more than a complainer—especially when I'm the one complaining. Of course, when I'm doing it, it's just "venting." I'm sure you understand.

I learned to be a Solver during my management career. My first position was as the leader of an outstanding team of computer technicians. Our award-winning team could fix any problem, whether it a broken computer or a frustrated customer. Lest I digress, I cannot express my gratitude enough for the patience, understanding, and lessons they gave me as a new manager. I can only sum it up by yelling "Whoo-ya!" They will understand. Anyway, we only had one or two complainers on the team but oh, what complainers they were!

I made the rookie mistake of trying to please everybody who complained. I just couldn't keep up. Finally, my mentor gave me some constructive feedback that I'll never forget. He said, "Why are you trying to fix all their problems? They know what they need to do. They can fix their problems better than you can!" Then he gave me the magic words that everyone should ask a complainer, "What do **you** think needs to be done?"

They will usually reply, "Nothing, I just wanted you to know." Problem solved. If they said, "I don't know, you're the boss," then I'd used the magic words. I insisted they think of a plan "A" and a backup plan "B". I would offer to help with a plan "C" that perhaps they never thought of. Problem solved. Finally, if they gave me a laundry list of what needed fixing I'd ask them to volunteer to lead a project to resolve the top three issues. After a while, they stopped complaining because they knew they would end up having to do something about it. Problem solved.

Yes, I'm oversimplifying to make a point and have a little fun. In fact, our company invested in a significant amount of training and high performance team development. As we learned and practiced together, our team became very good problem solvers. The complaints faded away, employee morale was the highest ever, and customer satisfaction soared. Problem solved!

Reflect on Purpose

Reflect on the following and discuss with **Your People:**

1. What is an Attitude of Purpose?
2. How have I used an Attitude of Purpose to help with my goals?
3. What do I enjoy doing for work and for pleasure?
4. What do I do best?
5. What activities set my soul on fire?
6. What would I miss doing if I couldn't do it anymore?
7. What things do I spend my money on?
8. Why did I choose my career?
9. Why do I live where I live?
10. Why do I spend time with the people I hang around?
11. Why am I dating or married to the person I'm with?
12. Why do I spend my free time the way I do?
13. If I had unlimited money, how would I spend my time?
14. What legacy do I want to leave?

	ATTITUDE OF POSSIBLITY
1	**Possibility Blockers**
2	Scotomas are blockers, they filter out your perception of the truth
3	Words can be blockers or enablers; choose encouraging words
4	**Possibility Zone**
5	Self-talk; choose positive and supportive words
6	Visualization; see yourself in action, experience all five senses
7	Affirmations; repeat daily as if you've already achieved the goal
8	Reticular Activating System; program the RAS, filter distractions
9	Uncomfortable Zone; imperfection is uncomfortable
10	Positive Wizard; empower others to believe in themselves
11	Possibility Wizard; help others see their unlimited potential
12	**Be a Possibility Wizard to Others—and to Yourself!**

ATTITUDE OF POSSIBILITY

An "Attitude of Possibility" is the belief that anything you want to do or become is possible. This section covers how to avoid "Possibility Blockers", get into your "Possibility Zone", and become a "Possibility Wizard" to others—and to yourself.

> *You've done it before and you can do it now. See the positive possibilities. Redirect the substantial energy of your frustration and turn it into positive, effective, unstoppable determination.*
>
> *—Ralph Marston*

Do you believe that anything is possible? Some people are optimistic about their future. They are confident in themselves, look forward to tomorrow with excitement, and generally take less time to recover from setbacks. Others are pessimistic about their future. They lack confidence, are fearful about what bad things may happen, and generally take longer to recover from failure. An optimist tends to attract more opportunities in life. A pessimist tends to repel opportunities.

According to a study by Kubzansky and Wright, optimism promotes an enhanced well-being whereas pessimism is a risk factor for poor health. Another study by Fredrickson concludes that a positive outlook produces health and success. Select an Attitude of Possibility for good health and great success!

> *The pessimist complains about the wind; the optimist expects it to change; the realist adjusts the sails.*
>
> —*William Arthur Ward*

Possibility Blockers

"Possibility Blockers" prevent us from seeing what is possible for our lives. They can lead to negative beliefs about ourselves and become our "truths". What we perceive often determines our attitude and behavior. We can change our negative attitude and behavior by changing the way we perceive the world.

> *We simply assume that the way we see things is the way they really are or the way they should be. And our attitudes and behaviors grow out of these assumptions.*
>
> —*Stephen R. Covey*

BLIND SPOTS. The brain works hard to filter out information it receives but doesn't need. It purposely impairs our mental vision to focus only on what is necessary at the time. An impaired mental vision is what Lou Tice calls a scotoma. Scotomas are mental blind spots that prevent you from seeing all of the the information needed to separate truth from fiction.

> *The obscure we see eventually. The completely obvious, it seems, takes longer.*
>
> —*Edward R. Murrow*

THE TRUTH. Did you notice a repeated word in the previous paragraph? It's in the sentence that starts with, "Scotomas are mental blind spots…" If not, then read it again. If you still can't find the repeated word, try reading the sentence backwards. If stumped, the answer is on the bottom of page 57. Did you have an "aha moment" when you saw it? This is an example of a scotoma preventing you from seeing the "truth". Have a little fun and see if **Your People** can find the repeated word!

> *The question is not what you look at, but what you see.*
>
> —*Henry David Thoreau*

PERCEPTION. Scotomas make the truth somewhat elusive at times. They limit our perception of the truth. The truth is not what's seen or heard; the truth is what you perceive it to be.

There is no truth. There is only perception.

—*Gustave Flaubert*

WORDS HAVE POWER. Words can be Possibility Blockers or Possibility Enablers. In her blog, *Harness The Power Of Words In Your Life*, social media consultant Barbara White agrees that we choose most words without thinking about what we are saying. We tend to be unaware of the positive or negative impact words have on other people. Words are powerful, so choose them thoughtfully.

We are masters of the unsaid words, but slaves of those we let slip out.

—*Winston Churchill*

WORDS HAVE EMOTION. Successful people are conscious of the words they use. They know the importance of choosing words that build self-esteem and confidence. They use words of affirmation, appreciation, and encouragement when speaking with others.

Words have a magical power. They can bring either the greatest happiness or deepest despair; they can transfer knowledge from teacher to student; words enable the orator to sway his audience and dictate its decisions. Words are capable of arousing the strongest emotions and prompting all men's actions.

—*Sigmund Freud*

PREVENT SCOTOMAS. **Your People** can help eliminate negative words and prevent scotomas. With a clear mental vision, and by using enabling words, you are more likely to see the unlimited possibilities for life.

It is a terrible thing to see and have no vision.

—*Helen Keller*

	POSSIBILITY ZONE
1	**Self-Talk**
2	The subconscious believes what you say; use supportive words
3	**Affirmations and Visualization**
4	Imagine success, use words that connect action with emotion
5	**Reticular Activating System (RAS)**
6	Program the RAS to discover greater success
7	**Uncomfortable Zone**
8	Acknowledge imperfection; take incremental risks, not reckless
9	**Wizards**
10	Positive Wizard; empowers others to believe in themselves
11	Possibility Wizard; the possibility of unlimited potential in others
12	**Overcome Your Possibility Blockers by Thinking Differently**

Possibility Zone

In his book, *Foundations of Psychology*, Dr. Klaus Holzkamp defines the "Possibility Zone" as the relationship between doing something instead of wondering if it's possible to do. You can get into the Possibility Zone by programming your mind to think differently.

> *We cannot solve our problems with the same thinking we used when we created them.*
>
> —*Albert Einstein*

THINK DIFFERENTLY. Try to keep an open mind while reading this section. Most successful people got that way by learning to think differently. You can too!

> *The secret of life is to have a task, something you devote your entire life to, something you bring everything to, every minute of the day for the rest of your life. And the most important thing is, it must be something you cannot possibly do.*
>
> —*Henry Moore*

HALF FULL. Possibility thinkers see the glass as half-full rather than half-empty. A half-empty glass has only the possibility of becoming completely empty. On the other hand, it's possible to fill a half-full glass to the brim, or adding even more to overflow it! You get the point. Be a possibility thinker and see the glass as half-full.

> *An optimist will tell you the glass is half-full; the pessimist, half-empty; and the engineer will tell you the glass is twice the size it needs to be.*
>
> —*Oscar Wilde*

IT'S RELATIVE. Circumstances may be positive or negative, but relative to what. Sure, things could always be better, but they could also be worse. Everything is relative to your perception of the truth. Don't allow Possibility Blockers to let you only see how a situation could be worse. Get in the Possibility Zone and see how a situation can be better!

> *Take your mind off the problems for a moment, and focus on the positive possibilities. Consider how very much you are able to do.*
>
> —*Ralph Marston*

WHY NOT? The words we choose are very powerful. Use words that are Possibility Enablers. Eliminate "no", and replace with "why not?"

> *Some people see things as they are and say 'Why?' I dream of things that never were and say 'Why not?'*
>
> —*George Bernard Shaw*

Self-Talk

Self-talk is the ongoing and unspoken conversation in the mind. The words chosen when talking to yourself can block or enable possibility thinking. Negative self-talk leads to a negative self-image, whereas positive self-talk builds a positive self-image. Self-talk can be your kindest supporter or harshest critic.

> *Every day, in every way, I'm getting better and better.*
>
> — *Émile Coué*

DON'T JOKE. You might make a mistake and call yourself dumb. You consciously don't mean it, but the subconscious doesn't know it's a joke, so don't do it!

Our subconscious minds have no sense of humor, play no jokes and cannot tell the difference between reality and an imagined thought or image. What we continually think about eventually will manifest in our lives.
— *Sidney Madwed*

MASTER YOURSELF. The subconscious records everything said as if it were fact. Instead of pointing out how dumb you are, encourage yourself by saying, "That's not like me. I'll do better the next time." Be your own kindest supporter with positive and supportive self-talk!

Self-suggestion makes you master of yourself.
— *W. Clement Stone*

DAILY MANTRAS	
1	**WHO:** "Am I being a Possibility Wizard to others and myself?"
2	**WHAT:** "What can I do right now that is more than expected of me?"
3	**WHEN:** "What's the best use of my time right now?"
4	**WHERE:** "Where am I going, and what's the worst that can happen?"
5	**WHY:** "Do the Right Thing!"
6	**HOW:** "Respond, don't react; stop, feel, think, act."
7	
8	**SELECT** my Attitude: What's my attitude right now?
9	**MANAGE** my Goals: Am I on track with my goals?
10	**INVEST** in Myself: What new education and training do I need?
11	**LIVE** a Balanced Life: What improvements can I make?
12	**EMBRACE** Change: Am I prepared for the next change that is coming?

DAILY MANTRAS. The daily mantras on the note card above is a list of self-talk I use every day. Whether using these examples, or creating your own, use positive and supportive self-talk. They can help your daily performance and success.

Relentless, repetitive self-talk is what changes our self-image.
— *Denis Waitley*

VISUALIZATION	
1	You Have the Ability to Program the subconscious
2	Keep an open mind because it can make a positive difference!
3	Routinely used by top performing athletes and successful people
4	See Yourself in Action
5	Not standing next to the car, you're looking from the driver's seat
6	Experience With All Five Senses
7	See, hear, feel, smell, taste
8	Feel the Emotion
9	Your heart is pumping with excitement; your mouth is watering!
10	Visualization is Very Different from Daydreaming
11	Daydreaming is just picturing what you want
12	Visualization is the first-person experience with all five senses

Visualization

You have the ability to program the subconscious to assist in achieving goals. It may seem strange at first, but keep an open mind because it can make a positive difference in your life. You program the subconscious mind by imagining success, or visualizing it, before it happens. Visualization is an effective technique routinely used by top performing athletes and other successful professionals.

> I believe that visualization is one of the most powerful means of achieving personal goals.
>
> —Harvey Mackay

DON'T DAYDREAM. Visualization is very different from daydreaming. Daydreaming is just thinking about what you want. In contrast, visualization is a first-person experience that connects actions with emotions. Random daydreaming is not effective, but visualizing success before you achieve it is powerful!

> Formulate and stamp indelibly on your mind a mental picture of yourself as succeeding. Hold this picture tenaciously. Never permit it to fade. Your mind will seek to develop the picture ... Do not build up obstacles in your imagination.
>
> —Norman Vincent Peale

SEE IT TO BELIEVE IT. The subconscious records everything you visualize as if it were fact. For example, the subconscious believes you're actually driving the new car. Then it creates the motivation within to take action to get it.

> *Visualize this thing that you want, see it, feel it, believe in it.*
> *Make your mental blue print, and begin to build.*
>
> —*Robert Collier*

KEY POINTS. The visualization process includes the following:

- SEE YOURSELF IN ACTION. You're not standing next to the new car. Instead, you're in the driver's seat, hands on the wheel and foot on the gas pedal.

- EXPERIENCE WITH ALL FIVE SENSES. You see the curve in the road ahead, hear the engine rev, feel the acceleration, enjoy that new car smell, and taste the salty air from the ocean nearby.

- FEEL THE EMOTION. Your heart is pumping, face is smiling, and mouth is watering with excitement. You love this new car!

S.M.I.L.E. VISUALIZATIONS	
1	**Select Your Attitude**
2	I'm sitting at my desk reading email ...
3	**Manage Your Goals**
4	I'm at my college graduation ceremony ...
5	**Invest in Yourself**
6	My boss is thanking me for a job well done ...
7	**Live a Balanced Life**
8	I'm playing in a resort pool with my family ...
9	**Embrace Change**
10	It's the first day of my new job ...
11	
12	

EXAMPLES. The following are examples of visualizations linking emotion and all five senses with action:

- SELECT YOUR ATTITUDE. I'm sitting at my desk reading email. I see my hands on the keyboard and the monitor in front of me. I notice an email from my boss about my project so I get excited. I hear the click as I open it. I feel like jumping for joy because it says my project is complete—on time and under budget! I can smell the aroma of that tender and juicy steak I'm going to reward myself with tonight!

- MANAGE YOUR GOALS. I'm at my college graduation ceremony, and I can feel the sense of anticipation and excitement as the names are announced. I hear my name, and my heart races! I walk to the stage, receive my diploma, and turn to get a picture taken while the dean is shaking my hand. I can smell the candles as I blow them out then bite into my favorite victory cake. Sweet, just like my accomplishment!

- INVEST IN YOURSELF. It's our morning staff meeting and we're all sitting at the conference table. The coffee smells great and the pastry is delicious. My boss calls my name and all eyes turn to me. I'm bursting with joy as she thanks me for a job well done. I hear the applause from the team, and that makes me feel much appreciated!

- LIVE A BALANCED LIFE. I'm playing with my family on a hot day in a resort swimming pool. The sound of happy children fills the air. My wife hands me a snack and a drink and tells me how much she loves me for adjusting my workload so we could have this vacation. The snack is salty, the drink is sweet, and both are awesome. Even more awesome is the love I feel from my family.

- EMBRACE CHANGE. It's the first day of my new job and I'm meeting with the boss. He is sitting in front of me and welcoming me to his team. I am so thankful to have this job. I take a cool drink of bottled water and I am excited for my future. The office has a pleasant smell of new furniture and fresh paint. Likewise, I now have a fresh start as I begin to build a relationship with my new boss.

AFFIRMATIONS	
1	**In the Now**
2	In the present tense, as if it's happening now.
3	**Be Positive**
4	Focus only on what you want, rather than what you don't want
5	**Be Concise**
6	Fewer words are easier to remember
7	**Include Action**
8	Affirm yourself as the person taking action
9	**Include Emotion**
10	It's crucial to use words that connect action with feelings
11	**Written Down**
12	On smartphone; repeat daily, read slowly, feel the emotion

Affirmations

You program the subconscious mind by repeating supportive words. Am I really suggesting that you talk to yourself? You already do with random thoughts, so why not do it intentionally and improve performance? This is a powerful technique routinely used by most successful people. In her best-selling book, *You Can Heal Your Life*, Louise L. Hay describes how to turn negative self-talk around into positive affirmations to "create a new experience for yourself."

> *Affirmations are statements going beyond the reality of the present into the creation of the future through the words you use in the now.*

> —*Louise L. Hay*

HEAR IT TO BELIEVE IT. Affirmations work by convincing yourself a goal has already been achieved. The subconscious is always working to maintain sanity. It doesn't separate fact from fiction so it believes what you imagine is the "truth". A negative self-image can be a barrier to success. A positive self-image can be very powerful. It can help achieve almost anything you imagine. The subconscious produces an inner motivation to match "truth" with reality. It affects actions, behavior, and choices to achieve or become what you affirm to be true.

You've probably heard the story about a rock in the road or may have experienced it. You're riding a bicycle down the road and suddenly see a rock. It's just the right size that if you were to hit it, then you could damage the wheel, upend the bike, and fall off. You stare at the rock trying to steer around it, but end up hitting it anyway. That's because you focused on the rock and the subconscious filtered out the path around it.

Conversely, the opposite is true. With more experience riding a bicycle, you learn to focus on the path to safety versus the rock in the road. Without realizing it, you're creating a self-image that the subconscious believes to be true. Then it automatically moves your muscles to steer away from the trouble ahead. Use visualization and affirmations to steer your life toward success!

> *Everything you do, every thought you have, every word you say creates a memory that you will hold in your body. It's imprinted on you and affects you in subtle ways—ways you are not always aware of. With that in mind, be very conscious and selective.*
>
> —*Phylicia Rashad*

CONFIDENTIAL. Written affirmations are things you want to achieve. They are personal and shouldn't be shared with people who don't need to know. Once change begins, then others may constantly remind you of what you were. Share personal affirmations only with **Your People** who understand how they work, and who can help you realize them faster.

> *If you reveal your secrets to the wind, you should not blame the wind for revealing them to the trees.*
>
> —*Khalil Gibran*

COMBINATIONS. Combining affirmations with visualization will yield the most positive result. Use all five senses as you picture yourself doing the action and feeling the emotion. Repeatedly affirm the words and pictures as truth in the subconscious. Your desire and motivation will grow from within, and you'll likely attract more success than you thought was possible.

> *Any thought that is passed on to the subconscious often enough and convincingly enough is finally accepted.*
>
> —*Robert Collier*

KEY POINTS. The key points of writing affirmations are:

- IN THE NOW. Write affirmations in the present tense, as if it's happening now.

- BE POSITIVE. Focus only on what you want, rather than what you don't want.

- BE CONCISE. Fewer words are easier to remember.

- INCLUDE ACTION. Affirm yourself as the person taking action.

- INCLUDE EMOTION. It's crucial to use words that connect action with your feelings.

- WRITTEN DOWN. Write affirmations on note cards, your smartphone, or somewhere you can easily access them.

- REPEATED OFTEN. To use written affirmations, pick a time or a few times per day when you can focus. Read each one slowly and be sure to feel the emotion connected with the action. Read aloud if alone, or silently in your mind if not. There ims no limit as to how many affirmations you write, other than the time it takes to read them.

S.M.I.L.E. AFFIRMATIONS	
1	**Select Your Attitude**
2	I'm proud of myself because I selected my attitude to ….
3	**Manage Your Goals**
4	I am an accomplished … because I set goals to do or become …
5	**Invest in Yourself**
6	I feel competent by developing my knowledge and skills in …
7	**Live a Balanced Life**
8	I am loved by my family, I did the right thing by …
9	**Embrace Change**
10	I'm excited for the future because I embrace change by …
11	
12	

EXAMPLES. The following are examples of present tense, positive affirmations that link emotion with action:

- SELECT YOUR ATTITUDE. I'm proud of myself because I selected my attitude, took a risk, and the email I'm reading reports my project is complete, on time and under budget.

- MANAGE YOUR GOALS. I am an accomplished college graduate because I managed my goals and earned the degree I see hanging on the wall in front of me.

- INVEST IN YOURSELF. I feel competent by developing my knowledge and skills on the job. I feel appreciated because my boss is thanking me for a job well done in the staff meeting we are attending right now.

- LIVE A BALANCED LIFE. I am loved by my family because I did the right thing to adjust my workload, and now we are in the resort pool enjoying our vacation together.

- EMBRACE CHANGE. I am excited for the future because I embraced a change of jobs. Now I have a fresh start as I begin to build a relationship with my new boss who is sitting in front of me.

Reticular Activating System

Reticular what? To some it may seem strange or technical, but this is a powerful concept and worth your utmost attention and consideration. I'll keep it as non-technical as possible with the hope that you'll use this potentially life-changing information to help accomplish goals faster and with fewer failures.

The reticular activating system, "RAS", is a part of the brain that receives information and filters out what you don't need. Could you imagine not having a RAS? The mind would be constantly bombarded with everything coming in from all five senses. For example, the eyes are looking straight-ahead reading this sentence, but they can still see the area to the left and right. The RAS is filtering out peripheral vision to focus on the words, instead of what's next to you. What do you see right now out of the corner of your eye? Now that you're thinking about it, your eyes might have suddenly moved off the page. That was the RAS in action.

The RAS filters out what's not important at the time, while allowing in what is important. That's great, but it can't separate fact from fiction, or positive from negative. Therefore, you'll want to program the RAS with positive things to look for so that it will automatically filter out the negatives.

For example, have you ever noticed while driving that one model car doesn't stand out from the others? Then when you decide to purchase a certain one, all of a sudden the same model is everywhere. Perhaps you've been to a party having an engrossing conversation. You're unaware of any specific sounds or people talking. Then someone across the room says your name and you hear it instantly. Another example is a new mother taking a nap with her baby in the other room. The noise of a nearby train doesn't disturb her but she wakes up instantly if the baby starts to cry. The RAS allows these examples to get through its filter because they are all valuable or threatening, and therefore important at the time.

Program your RAS with positive visualization and affirmations. Practice using both together and you may discover more success than ever imagined was possible. Use the RAS to stay in the Possibility Zone!

> *It is only through your conscious mind that you can reach the subconscious. Your conscious mind is the porter at the door, the watchman at the gate. It is to the conscious mind that the subconscious looks for all its impressions.*
>
> —Robert Collier

Uncomfortable Zone

Have you ever tried to do something new? How did it feel before you were about to try it? A new situation can be the "fear of the impossible", or the "thrill of the possible." Somewhere within these extremes is the comfort zone, uncomfortable zone, and danger zone.

> *If I were dying, my last words would be: Have faith and pursue the unknown end.*
>
> —Oliver Wendell Holmes, Jr.

COMFORT ZONE. The "Comfort Zone" is where you feel secure or in control. People who live here tend to have a fear of the impossible, whether they realize it or not.

> *The comfort zone is the great enemy to creativity; moving beyond it necessitates intuition, which in turn configures new perspectives and conquers fears.*
>
> —Dan Stevens

UNCOMFORTABLE ZONE. The "Uncomfortable Zone" is where you feel less secure or losing control. It's okay to be uncomfortable as you anticipate the thrill of the possible. Successful people tend to live in their Uncomfortable Zone. Living here usually results in breakthrough thinking, creativity, and innovation.

> *Move out of your comfort zone. You can only grow if you are willing to feel awkward and uncomfortable when you try something new.*
>
> —Brian Tracy

DANGER ZONE. The "Danger Zone" is where something doesn't feel right. You're aware that a situation could turn out very wrong if not careful. People living here tend to be either adventurous thrill-seekers, or scared to take risks.

> *Nothing in the world is more dangerous than a sincere ignorance and conscientious stupidity.*
>
> —Martin Luther King Jr

GET IN YOUR ZONE. The key points of how to get in the Uncomfortable Zone are:

- ACKNOWLEDGE IMPERFECTION. Be willing to look a little foolish or feel a little awkward when trying something new. For example, try using the sub-dominant hand for just one day and you'll get the idea. If right handed, try brushing your hair with the left hand. Acknowledge imperfection to gain new perspectives, build confidence, and overcome fears.

- INCREMENTAL RISKS. Start with small risks. Once you believe in the ability to manage them, then it will be easier to take on increasingly larger risks.

- RISK NOT RECKLESS. Don't confuse risk with being reckless and stupid. There's a difference between accepting risks and being reckless. Reckless people tend not to think about risks or consider the negative consequences. Consider the risks before acting. If you accept the risks, then accept the consequences if things don't work out as planned.

MANAGE YOUR ZONE. If you don't manage the Uncomfortable Zone then it will manage you. Don't be risk-averse and not even try to get what you want out of life.

> *To the degree we're not living our dreams, our comfort zone has more control of us than we have over ourselves.*
> — *Peter McWilliams*

GET UNCOMFORTABLE. Select an Attitude of Possibility and get uncomfortable as you enter the Possibility Zone!

> *Life begins at the end of your Comfort Zone. So if you're feeling uncomfortable right now, know that the change taking place in your life is a beginning, not an ending.*
> — *Neale Donald Walsch*

Wizards

POSITIVE WIZARD. A "Positive Wizard" empowers others to believe in themselves. Lou Tice coined this phrase after a 1939 musical fantasy movie, *The Wizard of Oz*. The story is about Dorothy with no home, the lion with no courage, the scarecrow with no brains, and the tin man with no heart. They all believed the Wizard could give them what they were missing. So they followed the yellow brick road as they sang, "We're off to see the Wizard, the wonderful Wizard of Oz." As it turns out, he wasn't a real wizard at all! He simply used the words "by the power vested in me…" which empowered them to believe in what they already had. Always remember that **you** are the Wizard to some people. Choose words carefully to influence the success of others— and yourself.

> *Think twice before you speak, because your words and influence will plant the seed of either success or failure in the mind of another.*
> — *Napoleon Hill*

NEGATIVE WIZARD. A "Negative Wizard" chooses hurtful and defeating words that demoralize others into not believing in themselves. A Negative Wizard says things like "Can't you do better?", "That sucks!", and "I knew you couldn't do it!" On the contrary, a Positive Wizard chooses kind and supportive words like, "Good job!", "That looks great!", and "I knew you could do it!"

> *We do not believe in ourselves until someone reveals that deep inside us something is valuable, worth listening to, worthy of our trust, sacred to our touch. Once we believe in ourselves we can risk curiosity, wonder, spontaneous delight or any experience.*
>
> —e. e. Cummings

POSSIBILITY WIZARD. A "Possibility Wizard" empowers others to believe in the unlimited potential to do or become whatever they want. Choose your attitude and self-talk to become a Possibility Wizard to others—and to yourself!

> *People become really quite remarkable when they start thinking that they can do things. When they believe in themselves they have the first secret of success.*
>
> —Norman Vincent Peale

Stories on Possibility

The following stories are on this section, *Attitude of Possibility*:

- Teaching Without a Voice
- You Get What You Expect
- Chuck-A-Puck
- Musical Imperfection
- No Regrets

Teaching Without a Voice

My teaching career in the Army started with a few surprises. I put on my freshly starched white lab coat and headed off to the classroom.

My first surprise came when I opened the door to the "meat locker." It was in the basement of a very old red brick building, and in the middle of winter. It was cold. The classroom was empty except for one short person standing there in civilian clothes. If it weren't for his matching lab coat, I would've thought he was the janitor.

My next surprise came when he introduced himself, "Hi, I'm Paul; you must be the new guy!" I was expecting a normal speaking voice, but what came out of his mouth was as if he was gargling his words to me. I shook his outstretched hand and for a moment, I suspected this was a joke on the "new guy." I noticed the stoma cover he was wearing over his neck, and now I was embarrassed. I just stood there for a moment, but he let me off the hook and gargled, "Throat cancer. Had my vocal chords removed." He reached up to the stoma cover and pinched a corner with two fingers, but didn't lift it. Then he grinned ear-to-ear and said, "Wanna see?" The shock on my face turned into laugher. We laughed together for what seemed like hours. In an instant, I made a new friend who soon became my teaching mentor.

Paul explained that a couple of years ago, he was a teacher who faced a future without a voice. After his laryngectomy, recovery was slow and painful. He wore a cover over his tracheostoma to avoid discomforting others. He was given a mechanical resonator he affectionately called "Robbie the Robot." He learned to hold Robbie next to his throat, and shape his mouth and lips to form words out of the vibrations.

I never fully understood how Paul felt. He was very proud and refused to complain, but on one rare occasion, he shared his frustration and embarrassment using Robbie. He was told he would never teach again because Robbie was too distracting for the students. I imagined his thoughts upon hearing this. What? What do you mean stop teaching? Get cancer; whatever! Surgery to remove larynx; piece of cake! Rehabilitate and learn to speak again; he was up to the challenge! But not teach again? Teaching was like breathing to Paul. His passion, his purpose. He couldn't—no wouldn't—do anything else!

My final surprise came when I learned what Paul's doctor said. His doctor told him that Robbie was his only option so Paul should just find another career. That wasn't going to happen. Paul entered his Possibility Zone on a mission to prove they were all wrong! He is a teacher—so that is what he is going to do!

The teacher became the student as Paul entered speech therapy to learn esophageal speech. He swallowed air and forced it up through his esophagus to produce a voice like a low-pitched burp. It's a very difficult and exhausting skill, but Paul was an "A" student.

Paul is an example of responding to an extraordinary setback with an Attitude of Possibility. He changed his life and the lives of many students, including myself. Thank you, Paul!

It was a privilege to learn from Paul, and I'm grateful I had him as a mentor. I will always remember his infectious and positive outlook on life. It always amazed me how he could lecture for hours on end—proving the possible—teaching without a voice.

Life is "beautimous!"

—Paul E. Bricker, Jr.

You Get What You Inspect

Every year we have the privilege at my company to receive feedback from our customers. The customer satisfaction survey provides an opportunity to look at our successes, review lessons learned, and make plans for continuous improvement. Years ago, the survey changed from a mail-in to an email process. Our headquarters, "HQ", received the email survey and forwarded a copy to the field office that serviced the customer. It became an overwhelming task to analyze hundreds of email messages and make any sense out of them. I had some computer programming training so I decided to see what I could to about the problem.

Armed with an Attitude of Possibility, I learned how to electronically scan the email and store the information in a database. Then I could run reports against the database and provide an analysis to management. Problem trends became clear as well as what resources and training was needed to improve our performance.

I showed it to my unit manager, and he loved the idea. As my mentor, he promoted it with our district manager who immediately called me. Without a hello she said, "Dreher!" By the way, everyone she loves she calls by his or her last name only. Then she asked only two questions, "What do you call it, and when can I have it?"

I signed up for a job and didn't even know it was coming! Now I had to have a name and a deadline for it. I explained it's for tracking the field annual survey. She said, "I know that. What do you call it?" Our company loves acronyms so I said, as more of a question than a response, "F.A.S.T. It stands for Field Annual Survey Tracker?" "I love it!" was her response. "Now when can I have it?" I was thinking aloud I could work on it over the weekend and maybe … "Perfect, I'll expect a presentation on Monday. See you later." Click. Actually, she is a very caring person and a mentor for me. She would never be rude; I'm just having a little fun with the story.

Our organization used the F.A.S.T. program to rise to the top in the country, as measured by the survey. Word of the program spread to other organizations, and one day I got a call from HQ. They said, "You can't do that." I replied, "We're already doing it and we're #1, but you already know that." Then I added, "Wouldn't the CEO be pleased if it could be used to improve customer satisfaction worldwide?" Name-dropping doesn't always work, but it did this time and soon I was on a plane to HQ. They adopted it, and I eventually moved on, leaving the F.A.S.T. program in good hands with a colleague who continued to improve it.

One day I was with the district manager and I asked why she insisted we post the F.A.S.T. reports and other operational metrics on the wall in the office. I'll always remember her response, "Dreher, You don't get what you EX-pect, only what you IN-spect." She explained, "The employees know what the metrics are. When you're tracking their progress and rewarding their success, then they become motivated to meet or exceed expectations." Yet another great life lesson from a great mentor!

In conclusion, I solved a problem with an Attitude of Possibility. I entered into my Possibility Zone, questioned the established norm, and contributed a new idea that had a significant impact to the company. As my mentor would say, "Dreher, you got what you IN-spected!"

You don't get what you expect, only what you inspect.
—Aggie Rucker

Chuck-A-Puck

My wife tells a great story at dinner parties about an experience we shared together and still laugh about today. It's a simple story that tells how we used an Attitude of Possibility to do even more than we knew was possible. We hope it's not only entertaining, but may inspire you to do the same for your community. We are active at our church and participate in fundraisers for helping the needy. Our local professional hockey team sponsors a fundraiser activity called "Chuck-a-Puck."

Local non-profit groups share in the winnings of a very fun game of chance on the ice. Fans purchase foam-rubber pucks from the non-profit groups. The number on the puck is recorded to identify the winner. At the end of the second period, the mascot and assistants skate out on the ice and place a large bullseye in the middle. Anticipation builds when the announcer invites the participants down to the glass. The crowd goes wild as they throw their pucks toward the bullseye with reckless abandon. The closest to the middle shares the winnings with the non-profit group.

The first time we did this, we sold the fewest pucks, and therefore we earned the least amount of the winner's share. Someone in our group sadly said, "We can't sell as many pucks as the other groups." You can probably guess what I replied, "Why not?" I had no idea how, but I was determined to figure it out. Suddenly I realized we were going about this the wrong way. I couldn't wait for the next opportunity to put my idea to the test!

I noticed that other groups sold only enough pucks that a participant could hold in their hands—usually one or two. They had long lines as each person filled out a registration card. The card assured the group would get their fair share of the winnings. We took a different approach.

Prior to that night, we had saved our recyclable grocery bags and brought stacks of them with us to the hockey arena. We organized our group to count out the pucks into bags of 5, 10, and 20. We asked them to pre-fill in the registration cards so all the participant had to do was write down their name and number. We had virtually no lines. Most everyone purchased the large bags of 20. The arena had to provide extra security to take all the cash to the office and two runners to go find more pucks from storage. We were having a great time hawking, "Chuck … A … Puck!" to the fans in about every way it was possible to pronounce the words. The fans had fun, we had fun, and we sold a record number of pucks!

We used an Attitude of Possibility to achieve success in a small way for ourselves, but in a big way for some of the needy in our community. All made possible with the money we raised playing the game of "Chuck-a-Puck!"

Musical Imperfection

Playing the piano was always a dream of mine. I tried a little in my teens, but I wasn't perfect so I gave up and learned to play guitar instead. Years later, I played in a church praise band. Eventually, the leader moved on and he took his piano skills with him. We had no piano player, no money to hire one, and I wasn't skilled enough to lead with guitar. Someone had to learn the piano, or we would revert to a traditional service with organ music. A traditional service is fine occasionally, but I have a passion for the upbeat and contemporary style of praise music. This really wasn't a decision, my passion made it for me.

I purchased a keyboard and was determined to learn how to play it. I quickly realized I didn't have the time to practice and become the next Billy Joel, my piano idol. I acknowledged my imperfection and, after a steep learning curve, I became the piano player for the praise band.

Incidentally, before I learned to play, our church needed a new piano. I was "volunteered" to select it and I negotiated a terrific deal on a used one. In a remarkable coincidence, Billy Joel played it at one of his concerts—and he signed it! Every time I sit at the piano and see his signature staring at me, it reminds me of my imperfection. It was intimidating at first but now it's an inspiration for me. I have come to enjoy my imperfection and so do the people who come to hear me play.

It is incredible what I can do when I acknowledge imperfection. I enjoy getting into my Uncomfortable Zone and try new things. Don't wait for me, choose to acknowledge imperfection and get into your Uncomfortable Zone right now. You too may be amazed with what is possible by acknowledging imperfection!

The pursuit of perfection often impedes improvement.
—George F. Will

No Regrets

Fred is a retired business manager who lives with a wonderful woman, and is father of three children, and grandfather of two. He enjoys family activities, golf, photography, landscaping, reading, and has a passion for history and learning. I've never been to the Land of Oz, but the most Positive Wizard I could ever imagine is my friend and mentor, Fred. Here is his story.

"Everything that I've ever done I did with a positive attitude because of my father. Dad would always remind me that getting mad never solved any problems. He would say that getting mad created two problems, 'getting mad and getting over it'.

When Dad died on my 18th birthday, it was the toughest day of my life. A huge crowd of friends and relatives were laughing and partying. I got super mad and cried. The wife of an older brother came out to console me. She explained that they were not celebrating his death, but rather were celebrating his life! She went on to say, 'He wanted you to be like him, always positive and happy. It makes them feel good having known him. You should celebrate him also!' That day was so impactful that I will always find the good in any situation, no matter how bad it may seem. When you see the positive in your circumstances then you have no regrets about your choices.

I believe people start out good at heart, so I treat them with kindness, respect, and dignity, no matter who they are. No one is born negative. No one gets up in the morning to plan how to be miserable and fail. That's why I always talk to people and stress the positive. Just saying 'hello' can be uplifting to someone. If I didn't say anything, then they would walk by with head down to avoid contact. Instead, they will smile back, and I feel good about having a positive impact on them, at least for a moment.

My job as a manager was to make everyone under me as successful and happy as possible. As a leader, I would focus on what people do well. Everyone has different talents and personalities. Instead of browbeating them with what they did poorly, I stressed what they could do well.

Most of my career was in computer services. I had a few on my team that could not be great technicians, but had other talents. I would give them customers on whom they could make a positive influence. I had a couple of employees who were especially poor at fixing computers. What they lacked in skills, they made up with their persuasive personality. They were 'BSers' extraordinaire! They didn't have what it took to fix technical problems, but they could convince other people of almost anything. They made their contribution to the team by turning volatile customers around.

I guess it all goes back to personal philosophy. The goal is to be happy. I would ask myself how this person is going to be the happiest. After all, how can anyone not be successful it they are happy? It does not matter what someone wants, love money, or whatever. No one's goal is to be miserable. I've said the same thing to all of my children. Even in my role of 'father of the bride' speech at their weddings. You have to accept people for what they are, not what you want them to be. You need to find someone whose traits you can accept, because you can't change them. Whatever you may do in life, or whomever you marry, strive for happiness. Live your life without regrets."

Concern is constructive. Worry is destructive.

—*Fred Fernandez*

Reflect on Possibility

Reflect on the following and discuss with *Your People:*

1. What is an Attitude of Possibility?
2. How have I used an Attitude of Possibility to help with my goals?
3. What Possibility Blockers have I experienced?
   a. Why did they occur?
   b. How did I get around them?
4. What does "get into my Possibility Zone" mean?
   a. Do I ask "why" or "why not?"
   b. How do I use possibility thinking in my life?
5. What examples of self-talk do I consciously choose?
6. How have I used Visualization and Affirmations to help my performance or achieve a goal?
7. If I haven't tried using Visualization and Affirmations, am I willing to get into my Uncomfortable Zone and try them?
8. Describe a situation how my RAS prevented me from seeing the obvious?
9. When has my RAS helped me see something not as obvious?
10. Do I live in my Comfort Zone or Uncomfortable Zone?
11. How do I get into my Uncomfortable Zone and use it to stimulate creativity or innovation?
12. How I am a Possibility Wizard to myself? Am I to others?

(The repeated word in the sentence on page 34 is "the the")

ATTITUDE OF ACCOUNTABILITY	
1	**Responsibility**
2	Own a commitment to the results before you act
3	**Empowerment**
4	"Make it happen" and accept responsibility for the outcome
5	**Accountability**
6	Accept the consequences when you succeed or fail—good or bad
7	Be accountable for what you do first, then hold others accountable
8	Eliminate the "buts" and be accountable for your own destiny
9	**Motivation**
10	"Want to" versus "have to" attitude
11	**Resilience**
12	Bounce back from adversity with the support of *Your People*

ATTITUDE OF ACCOUNTABILITY

How does it feel to be accountable for something you're about to do? Are you afraid and threatened, or do you feel anticipation and excitement? Many people have learned to associate accountability with punishment. Others have learned to associate accountably with opportunity. Successful people believe that accountability is an opportunity for success.

> *I was seldom able to see an opportunity until it had ceased to be one.*
>
> —*Mark Twain*

MOTIVATION. An "Attitude of Accountability" is the responsibility (before), empowerment (during), and accountability (after) for your actions. In his worldwide best seller, *The Seven Habits of Highly Effective People*, management expert Stephen R. Covey describes how accountability creates self-motivation. Motivation combines responsibility, empowerment, and accountability into a burning desire for success. You're "on fire" when motivated, and nothing can stop you from achieving goals!

> *Motivation is a fire from within. If someone else tries to light that fire under you, chances are it will burn very briefly.*
>
> —*Stephen R. Covey*

Responsibility

RESPONSIBILITY IS A CHOICE. Responsibility is the belief that success or failure depends on what you do, or don't do. You own a commitment to the results before acting. Sometimes you accept sole responsibility for the results. Other times you accept shared responsibility with the team. In either case, responsibility is a choice to accept the consequences before you act.

> *Freedom is the will to be responsible to ourselves.*
> — *Friedrich Nietzsche*

Empowerment

EMPOWERMENT IS A CHOICE. Empowerment gives you the authority to act. You empower yourself and take the actions and risks necessary to achieve results. Rather than waiting for someone to declare you empowered, you "make it happen" and accept responsibility for the outcome.

> *Be miserable. Or motivate yourself. Whatever has to be done, it's always your choice.*
> — *Wayne Dyer*

Accountability

ACCOUNTABILITY IS A CHOICE. Accountability is taking the responsibility for the outcome of your actions, behaviors, and choices. Personal accountability means to accept the consequences of your choices whether they succeed or fail. A person who is accountable doesn't make excuses and won't assign blame on others.

> *Too often in life, something happens and we blame other people for us not being happy or satisfied or fulfilled. So the point is, we all have choices, and we make the choice to accept people or situations or to not accept situations.*
> — *Tom Brady*

ACCOUNTABILITY IS SHARED.   Accountability is a two-way street. First, be accountable for what you do.   Then, people will respect your confidence and self-esteem when you hold them accountable.   There is a line between having confidence and being overbearing.   Once you learn where the line is, avoid crossing it.

> *Life is not accountable to us. We are accountable to life.*
> —*Denis Waitley*

NO BUTS. Using "buts" leaves an out, and some amount of blame for others to make yourself feel better. For example, "I know I didn't pre-pare enough, **but** the other person was not open to my idea." Instead, be accountable by saying, "I know I didn't prepare enough so I'll try a different approach and win them over next time." Eliminate "buts" and take control of your destiny.

> *The only limits to the possibilities in your life tomorrow are the buts you use today.*
> —*Les Brown*

Motivation

MOTIVATION IS A CHOICE. Motivation is the desire to do things. It's a "want to" versus "have to" attitude. You want to succeed because you're responsible for choices, empowered to take action, and account-able for the results.

> *Want-to, Choose-to, Like-it, Love-it!*
> —*Lou Tice*

Resilience

RESILIENCE IS A CHOICE. Sometimes a setback occurs that, in hind-sight, you may have been able to prevent by making different choices. Other times a setback is unpreventable. There is no way to understand why it happened, or what you could've done to prevent it. Whether preventable or not, you can always choose how to respond to setbacks.

> *The ultimate measure of a man is not where he stands in moments of comfort and convenience, but where he stands at times of challenge and controversy.*
> —*Martin Luther King Jr.*

SUPPORT OF OTHERS. As a reminder, **Your People** include personal and professional resources. Personal relationships with loving people may be all you need for support. In addition, professional resources such as advisors, attorneys, and physicians are there for you if necessary. Sometimes it can be difficult, but with the support of **Your People**, it's possible to be resilient and bounce back from adversity.

> *God grant me the serenity to accept the things I cannot change; courage to change the things I can; and wisdom to know the difference.*
>
> —*Reinhold Niebuhr*

Stories on Accountability

The following stories are on this section, *Attitude of Accountability*:

- Escalate Early and Often
- Following the Money
- In It to Win It

Escalate Early and Often

An important part of my management career was to conduct an annual performance appraisal, "PA", with my team members. My philosophy for the PA is that accountability is a two-way street. My team was accountable for their performance, and I was accountable to them for my leadership. I adopted three guiding principles from my mentors for both my team and myself: do the right thing, no surprises, and no Friday escalations.

Do the right thing means to learn what the right thing to do is in each situation for others and for yourself—then do it! These four simple words effectively summed up the entire company policy and procedure manual. I used these words often with excellent results.

No surprises means to keep each other informed so there aren't any surprises during the PA. I grew up believing that if you don't make any mistakes then you aren't trying hard enough. Mistakes are forgivable, but accountability and action to improve is rewardable!

No Friday escalations mean that I value weekends away from work for both my team and myself. Most problems develop early in the week. They continue if someone doesn't follow the escalation procedure: get assistance from the team and give me a heads-up. By the end of the week, the customer's patience has run out and I get a phone call on Friday just before closing. Now we're in react mode. We spend the weekend working an issue that could've been resolved before affecting the customer's time off, and ours. A Friday escalation is a very bad thing. It won't be a surprise when it comes up during a PA.

I've always kept my boss informed to avoid Friday escalations. I let my boss know when I've done something well, and when I make mistakes. I work with my boss to figure out what I can do better the next time. That's how I like to be treated and how I tend to treat others. I do as the company says, "Escalate early, and escalate often!"

> *Every little thing is important. If you can correct the little, small things, you don't have them being escalated to the point where they become an issue.*
> —*Donnie Henderson*

Following the Money

Chris is married and just changed his career path to work for a large computer company. He enjoys spending time with his wife, has an appetite for rigorous exercise, and a passion for anything related to film and filmmaking, specifically in the area of editing. He has learned to select his attitude, set goals, adapt with change, and accept personal accountability for choices in different ways. Here is his story.

"I like to have a lot of energy and fun in everything I do. I got my positive mental attitude from my mother and a hard work ethic from my father. I have an older brother, who was a bit of a troublemaker, but I've avoided his example and we've both turned out well. I live my life having a daily goal, with time for work and time for home. I love work but I **cherish** my time off. There are people who make work their number one priority, but I don't want work to overflow into my personal life. I enjoy spending time with my wife, having fun.

I like seeing the bigger picture where I'll be in 5-10 years. I like to have a goal in mind and not just do what other people do. Success is different to everyone whether it's money, happiness, or whatever. The important part is having a goal in mind. Envision where you want to be and how to get there. It can be hard for young people to figure out their life in general. They can do it if they take the time to figure it out and don't give up too soon, otherwise they may regret not doing what they really want. Some people set unrealistic goals, for example, not everyone can be a famous musician. They should pursue their passion but shouldn't invest their entire life in one thing. Go for it and pursue your passion, but keep realistic and achievable goals. I don't want to be like some older people on their deathbed with a list of regrets.

The biggest change I've experienced in my life was before my marriage. My girlfriend traveled to Korea to teach English for one year. I didn't like the fact that she would be gone, but I wanted to support her to make her goals. I knew she would return in a year so it made it easier to accept. We adapted by using technology to Skype often and I visited her in Korea three times that year. Since she's been home, we married and she moved into my tiny studio apartment until we found a bigger place. Merging two lives and histories in one space was difficult but rewarding. I figured if we can live in one room for eight months then we can deal with anything.

Forever, I wanted to be a film editor. However, instead of going to school immediately and following that goal, I made the choice of following the money instead. Cellphone sales were killer in the mid 2000's. I was making two or three times what my college graduate friends were making. The consequence of my actions was that I went to school late and lost the passion I had when I graduated high school. I played it safe and got a degree that relates to my experience in sales rather than what makes me happy. So now what do I have to show for it? I have nine years of sales experience that has done me no good in reaching the goals I deep down wanted to achieve. I can only imagine what an amazing film editor I would have become had I spent the time doing that instead of following the money.

So, I'm dealing with these consequences and holding myself accountable by pursuing those other passions of mine in my spare time. I can't just give up and quit my job to become an editor, or make a small film. If I really want something, I have to make it happen and not just let it happen. I have to make time to see these become a reality. This is why I cherish my free time so much. During my free time, I watch editing how-to videos, study film after film, and learn all the aspects of making my own. One day, you'll see me at a film festival."

I like to have a lot of energy and fun with everything I do.
— Christopher McLaughlin

In It to Win It

Shak is a former entrepreneur who recently joined a large technology corporation. He enjoys spending time with his wife and their baby son. He has a strong family support system that gives him passion for success. Shak tells how he selects his attitude, sets goals, adapts with change, and accepts personal accountability for choices. Here is his story.

"My attitude revolves around the south Asian family concept of how everything is for the betterment of the family. My education, training, and work experience is based on what I can do to help them.

I believe that you can't do everything by yourself. You can get more done with the help of others. I know I would not be as successful without the team who supports me. Everyone has their own interpretation of what success is. Regardless, you have to keep focus on goals. Envision yourself at that point in time, backtrack, look at timelines, and implement steps to hit checkpoints. I know it is challenging, but if there is something you don't know, then learn how to do it.

Young people are ambitious and want to do great things, but they tend to reinvent the wheel. They say, "I want to do it my way." Humans have a lot of knowledge in books and experienced people. Friends and family have lived a longer life, so learn what to do, and what not to do, from them. Look at friends, parents, brothers, and sisters. Learn from their mistakes, follow the formula, and achieve success.

When I was eight years old, my family immigrated from India to America where I started second grade in Georgia. At sixteen, Dad saw that I loved technology so he moved the family to the heart of the Silicon Valley in California where I could pursue my interest. My brother is two years younger than I am. I have a sense of responsibility to guide him and to set an example as a role model. I knew that someday I wanted to marry and have children by a certain age. I set the vision and timeline, worked backwards, and set things in motion to meet checkpoints along the way. I always keep in mind my brother is watching. I want his mindset that he too can decide what he wants and to make plans to pursue his goals. I now have a family of my own so my focus has switched from my brother to my wife and child. I'm very happy with my new family and proud of being a positive role model for my brother.

My father was a politician in India where I was born. Dad and Mom have eight siblings each so I have a lot of cousins from different age groups. We grew up in an environment where you had to get along which helped me adapt to our move to America when I was eight years old. I learned English from the British, but that is not the same language spoken in my new country so I had to adapt to American English.

Speaking of changes, getting married and having a child in the same year was a big one! I like to plan and think of options, but all that stuff goes out the window after you have a child. Things become in focus that you never thought of before. As humans, we tend to react to situations, so when a child cries we react to do whatever is necessary. We put them first and try to stay positive. We adapt with preventive planning such as baby proof our house. Our son will be two years old this year and I couldn't be happier with my wife or prouder of our son!

Dropping out of college was big and has had an ongoing impact in my life. After a shakeup in the IT industry, my parents lost their job. I am the oldest in the family so I had to step up. I left college to pursue work so that I could help my family. I had a fulltime job in school as a sales trainer for a major wireless carrier. I used that experience to open three stores of my own. It was costly to stock inventory and stressful to make payroll, but the experience proved to be challenging and rewarding.

When the market declined, I looked for a new job. Prospective employers saw that my education was incomplete and they questioned my ability to commit. Fortunately, my experience was more important with one employer and I was finally able to land a great job with a huge technology corporation."

Challenges can be overcome when everyone is in it to win it.
There is always a way we can come up with solutions.
—*Shakeb Kundiwala*

Reflect on Accountability

Reflect on the following and discuss with ***Your People:***

1. What is an Attitude of Accountability?
2. How have I used an Attitude of Accountability to help me with my goals?
3. When have I accepted responsibility before starting a task or goal? How did it work out?
4. What does "own a commitment to the result" mean?
5. When was I part of a team and assigned responsibility? What was the outcome?
6. When have I felt empowered to take action? What were the results?
7. When have I demonstrated accountability for my actions? How did it make me feel?
8. When have I held someone else accountable for their actions? What happened?
9. Have I ever blamed someone else for something that caused me to fail?
10. When have I felt motivated with a "want to" versus "have to" attitude? What were the results?
11. When have I had a setback and was resilient enough to bounce back from it?

ATTITUDE OF GRATITUDE	
1	**Be Grateful**
2	Be thankful for what you have; grateful for what happens
3	Don't compare; you have more than you may realize
4	Success comes to those who appreciate what they already have
5	Have perspective; don't take the good times for granted
6	Optimism gives us the resilience to bounce back
7	Choose actions, behavior, and words of appreciation
8	**Pass it On**
9	Give of yourself without expecting anything in return
10	Give more than is needed of your time, talent, and treasure
11	Greed is the enemy of success
12	Generosity is contagious; be a positive influence on others

ATTITUDE OF GRATITUDE

Do you ever feel that you don't have enough time, money, or possessions? Conversely, do you ever ask how much is enough? Will it ever be enough? By the time you get it, it's not worth what it used to be. An "Attitude of Gratitude" is to be thankful for what you have, and grateful for what happens. There are good reasons to be grateful. A study by Emmons and McCullough conclude that expressing gratitude may have a positive impact on our mental and physical well-being, and interpersonal relationships. We express an Attitude of Gratitude with our thoughts, words, and actions.

> *Thankfulness is the beginning of gratitude. Gratitude is the completion of thankfulness. Thankfulness may consist merely of words. Gratitude is shown in acts.*
> —Henri Frederic Amiel

DON'T COMPARE. You may not have as much money or "stuff" as other people, but you don't have as many problems as they have. They have issues hanging on to it, taking care of it, and trying to get more of it. Only you can decide how much is enough, and if you want to deal with the problems that come with it.

> *Be thankful for what you have; you'll end up having more. If you concentrate on what you don't have, you will never, ever have enough.*
>
> —*Oprah Winfrey*

BE THANKFUL. Even if it's not as much as you want, there is still more than you may realize. A home may be smaller than you want, but it's comfortable and has lower property taxes. A car may be older, but it's affordable and reliable. Finally, you may have the most priceless and irreplaceable thing in the world—people who love and care about you! Be thankful for all you have. Success comes to those who appreciate what they already have. They can embrace what the future has in store for them, in good times and bad.

> *We can complain because rose bushes have thorns, or rejoice because thorn bushes have roses.*
>
> —*Abraham Lincoln*

HAVE PERSPECTIVE. It's easy to be grateful for the good things that happen, but how can you be grateful for the bad things, and why should you? Bad things aren't necessarily what you're grateful for, it's what they make you do or see that can be beneficial. Society tends to remember bad things. For example, many holidays honor fallen heroes. Remembering bad times puts things in perspective so that we do not take good times for granted. It's not about reliving the experience as much as gaining a new perspective, learning from it, and using it to create a better future.

> *We are made wise not by the recollection of our past, but by the responsibility for our future.*
>
> —*George Bernard Shaw*

BE OPTIMISTIC. Gratitude helps us appreciate what we have and live a more fulfilling life. Overcoming difficult challenges with an Attitude of Gratitude builds up our psychological immune system. It cushions us when we fall, and gives us the resilience to bounce back. We are grateful we made it through the bad times so we can be optimistic about the future.

> *Develop an attitude of gratitude, and give thanks for everything that happens to you, knowing that every step forward is a step toward achieving something bigger and better than your current situation.*
>
> —*Brian Tracy*

BE GRATEFUL. Choose the action, behavior, and words of appreciation that are appropriate to the situation. It will show thankfulness and gratitude to others—and to yourself!

> *Too often we underestimate the power of a touch, a smile, a kind word, a listening ear, an honest compliment, or the smallest act of caring, all of which have the potential to turn a life around.*
>
> —*Leo Buscaglia*

Pass it On

Pass what on? What is "it"? There are many words to describe "it": advice, compassion, compliments, empathy, forgiveness, generosity, gratitude, humility, kindness, knowledge, philanthropy, possibility, thankfulness, thoughtfulness, talent, time, treasure, wisdom, and more. "It" doesn't have to cost anything, or take much time, and can be easy to do. I'm talking about **you**! "Pass it On" means to give of yourself to others, without expecting anything in return.

> *We make a living by what we get. We make a life by what we give.*
>
> —*Winston Churchill*

GENEROSITY. Virtually all academic, religious, and scientific studies on generosity find that it is better to give than to receive. Most people who give a portion of their time, talent, and treasure will end up receiving even more in return.

The more generous we are, the more joyous we become. The more cooperative we are, the more valuable we become. The more enthusiastic we are, the more productive we become. The more serving we are, the more prosperous we become.
—*William A. Ward*

GIVE FREELY. Give more than is needed without expecting anything in return. If you have only a little, then give a little. If you have a lot, then give accordingly.

Think of giving not as a duty but as a privilege.
—*John D. Rockefeller, Jr.*

GREED. Greed is the enemy of success. Greedy people can temporarily "get ahead" in life, but tend not to live a happy and fulfilling one.

Greed is a bottomless pit, which exhausts the person in an endless effort to satisfy the need without ever reaching satisfaction.
—*Erich Fromm*

CONTAGIOUS. Being generous is a good example for others to follow. Select an Attitude of Gratitude and become a positive influence to some, and a role model to others. Be contagious to others with your generosity.

Practicing an attitude of gratitude spills over to acts of generosity.
—*Debbie Macomber*

NO REGRETS. When we give of ourselves, it would be nice if others would do the same. However, we can't expect it. Pass it On means to accept that some people cannot, or choose not, to do the same. Therefore, expecting it of others may lead to frustration and regret.

You give but little when you give of your possessions. It is when you give of yourself that you truly give.
—*Kahlil Gibran*

Grateful Service

"Grateful Service" is what we give to others with an Attitude of Gratitude. We're thankful for the opportunity to serve, and grateful for the experience. Grateful Service has its rewards—what we give to others and what we get in return.

> *The best way to find yourself is to lose yourself in the service of others.*
>
> —*Mahatma Gandhi*

PUT OTHERS FIRST. My professional life has largely been in computer services, where good customer service is expected. My social life includes many volunteering and service activities. In my personal life, I strive to serve my family not because I have to, but because I want to. People rarely expect much and they usually appreciate what I do for them. I always get something unexpected in return: challenging work, appreciation from others, and love from my family. I am grateful for the opportunity to serve others.

> *Put people first. Add value to people. They'll come back and add value to you. Serve people. They'll come back and serve you.*
>
> —*John Maxwell*

	GRATEFUL CUSTOMER SERVICE
1	**Select an Attitude of Gratitude**
2	Thankful for job, grateful for problems, make a good impression
3	**Listen First, Then Communicate**
4	Customers need to be heard and they need communication
5	**Do the Right Thing**
6	You will learn what the right thing to do is, so do it!
7	**Don't Take it Personally**
8	Remain calm but committed to make it right
9	You may have had no control over what went wrong
10	Learn stress management techniques; diet, exercise, meditation
11	Don't lose sleep by stressing over problems
12	**Provide Grateful Customer Service for Success!**

Grateful Customer Service

We all have customers in our professional life. We choose to get along with customers and meet or exceed their expectations. Some are internal and others are external to our organization. Internal customers are colleagues and bosses. External customers are those who pay for the services we provide. "Grateful Customer Service" is serving customers with an Attitude of Gratitude.

> *Customers don't expect you to be perfect. They do expect you to fix things when they go wrong.*
>
> —*Donald Porter*

KEY POINTS. The key points of providing Grateful Customer Service are:

- SELECT AN ATTITUDE OF GRATITUDE
  - BE THANKFUL. Customers are the reason you have a job. Tell them, "Thank you."
  - BE GRATEFUL. Problems are opportunities to retain and grow your customer base. Show your gratitude with an Attitude of Accountability to meet or exceed their expectations.
  - MAKE A GOOD IMPRESSION. Be mindful of your appearance, words, and body language.
- LISTEN FIRST, THEN COMMUNICATE
  - NEEDS AND WANTS. Set customer expectations on what they'll receive for what they've paid. Give them what they need (paid for), not always what they want (not paid for). Don't say "no" if they ask for more. Instead, explain what you need in order to give them what they want. Say "yes" without saying "no" by choosing words carefully. For example, "I can do what you want if I have more time." Or, "I can do what you want for a reasonable fee." The key is to start with a positive phrase like, "I can do that", versus a negative phrase like, "No, you didn't pay for that."
  - CUSTOMERS NEED COMMUNICATION. Customers are fair and forgiving if you tell them what's happening to resolve problems. Call them first (proactive) before they call you (reactive). Do this more than necessary until they let you

know how much communication is enough. You probably have only a few customer issues going at the same time, so keeping them informed should be manageable. If not, then ask your boss for assistance.

- CUSTOMERS WANT TO BE HEARD. Listen without inter-rupting. Remain calm and let them vent if necessary. Re-member, they are upset at the situation, not you. Repeat what you hear back to them. This confirms you heard them and understand the issue. For example, "What I'm hearing you say is that our invoice wasn't correct, please tell me more."

- CHOOSE YOUR WORDS. Note the words in the previous sentence: "our invoice" versus "your invoice." "Our" im-plies "our company" made a mistake, whereas "your" implies the customer made the mistake. Even if they did, disarm the situation by saying "our" problem. Then say "we", implying "our company," will get the issue resolved. Avoid saying "I" unless you personally did something to create the issue or failed to resolve it.

- ACCOUNTABILITY. By selecting an Attitude of Accountabil-ity, you'll be empowered to provide Grateful Customer Ser-vice, as well as accountable to resolve problems. Fix "our" issues first before holding the customer accountable for what they did, or did not do, to create or prolong the problem.

- DO THE RIGHT THING
    - You will learn what the right thing to do is, so do it!

    - Apologize for the situation and take their side when appro-priate to do so. For example, "I'm sorry our invoice wasn't correct. This situation is unacceptable! It certainly frustrates me when my cell phone bill is wrong. Tell me what we can do to make it right."

- DON'T TAKE IT PERSONALLY
    - Remain calm but committed to make it right.

- Most of the time, you personally had no control over what went wrong. The customer is not upset at you, the employee; they need your company to fix the problem.

- Learn stress management techniques including diet, exercise, and meditation. Ask **Your People** for tips on how to let it go and avoid stress.

- Don't lose sleep by stressing over customer problems. The problems won't go away and there is nothing you can do overnight. Get some rest because you'll need it. The problems will still be there tomorrow, but a fresh mind brings a fresh approach and new solutions.

- For example, try falling asleep while visualizing a calm and peaceful scenario. One I use is the "Beach Stroll". It's a moonlit evening and I'm slowly walking along a beach. I'm alone with no one in sight. I see the peaceful ocean (void of boats and people), feel the cool breeze, hear the gentle waves lap against the shore, and smell the fresh salty air. I think of nothing to stimulate my heart rate. I force my thoughts to stay focused on this picture and not think about anything else. By focusing on one thing only, my subconscious filters out the problems and allows me to drift off to sleep. It took some practice, but now it's rare for me to lose sleep over problems in my personal or professional life. Choose a scenario that works for you and get a good night's rest.

GRATEFUL SERVICE. Select an Attitude of Gratitude and provide Grateful Customer Service for success!

> *A customer is the most important visitor on our premises. He is not dependent on us. We are dependent on him. He is not an interruption in our work. He is the purpose of it. He is not an outsider in our business. He is part of it. We are not doing him a favor by serving him. He is doing us a favor by giving us an opportunity to do so.*
>
> *—Mahatma Gandhi*

	BE A GRATEFUL SERVER
1	**Professional**
2	Customers are the reason for your job
3	Problems are opportunities to retain and grow your customer base
4	You wouldn't have a job if there were no customers or problems
5	**Social**
6	Research volunteer organizations, find a match for your skills
7	Don't overcommit, bring an Attitude of Possibility, have fun!
8	**Personal**
9	Give your resources (time, talent, treasure) generously
10	Put the needs of your family and friends ahead of your wants
11	Be grateful to all—including yourself!
12	**A Grateful Server Provides Service with an Attitude of Gratitude**

Be a Grateful Server

Most of us provide service to customers in our professional life, service to others in our social life, and service to family and friends in our personal life. A "Grateful Server" serves others with an Attitude of Gratitude.

KEY POINTS. The key points of being a Grateful Server are:

- PROFESSIONAL. Customers, both internal and external, are the reason for your job. Problems are opportunities to retain and grow your customer base. You wouldn't have a job if there were no customers to serve, or no problems to solve.

- SOCIAL. Do your research on the volunteer organization. Find a match for your passion and skills, and don't overcommit. Remember that volunteering is different from a job and may require a different attitude. Bring an Attitude of Possibility and your sense of humor as well. Above all else, be enthusiastic and enjoy the experience!

- PERSONAL. Service to family and friends is giving your resources (time, talent, treasure) generously, putting their needs ahead of your wants, and being grateful to all—including yourself.

BE A GRATEFUL CUSTOMER	
1	**Do Your Research**
2	Learn the value of the product or service, not just the price
3	**Set Your Own Expectations**
4	In proportion to the value received
5	**Address Problems in a Constructive Manner**
6	Be calm; escalate in proportion
7	Give them a chance to make it right
8	**Reward and Recognize Grateful Customer Service**
9	Reward with money and gifts when appropriate
10	Recognize the server with praise in person, manager, or online
11	Reward and recognize with a simple "thank you"
12	**Select an Attitude of Gratitude and be a Grateful Customer!**

Be a Grateful Customer

We've read how to be a Grateful Server and how to provide Grateful Customer Service. Now let's switch roles from being a server to being the customer. Do your part to be a good customer. In fact, you can choose to be a "Grateful Customer".

> *The golden rule for every business man is this: Put yourself in your customer's place.*
>
> —*Orison Swett Marden*

IN PROPORTION. Does it bother you when a customer yells at a fast food server? It really irks me because something usually happened completely out of the server's control. This behavior is not in proportion to the value received and is unacceptable.

When I go to a restaurant owned by a chain and I pay under a certain amount, then I expect customer service that is acceptable, but no more. I address a problem if I think it will actually help the server or the restaurant. I may smile and politely say something to the server, or I may calmly escalate to the manager—but always in proportion to what I received. For example, the server may be excellent, but the food not so much. I reward the server and speak with the manager about the food.

When I go to an expensive restaurant, I expect high value with excellent food and service. If not, then I'll always escalate in proportion. The only exception is when I'm not the paying the bill. In that case, I try to keep my opinions to myself. However, I cannot claim to be perfect as my friends and family can attest.

Select an Attitude of Gratitude and be a Grateful Customer!

Nothing taken for granted, everything received with gratitude, everything passed on with grace ... I would maintain that thanks are the highest form of thought; and that gratitude is happiness doubled by wonder.

—*G.K. Chesterton*

KEY POINTS. The key points of being a Grateful Customer are:

- Do your research
    - Know the value of the product or service; it's more than just the price
    - Know what services you'll receive, and their limitations and exclusions
- Set your own expectation in proportion to the value received
    - Low-value means acceptable service
    - Mid-value means good service
    - High-value means excellent service
- Address problems in a constructive manner
    - State the issue clearly and in a calm voice
    - Give them a chance to make it right
    - Escalate in proportion to the value received
- Reward and recognize Grateful Customer Service
    - Reward with money and gifts when appropriate, or a simple "thank you"
    - Thank the server and their manager; or online with email and social media

Stories on Gratitude

The following stories are on this section, *Attitude of Gratitude*:

- Prove Them Wrong
- One Step at a Time
- Far Enough

Prove Them Wrong

Nick is a top sales representative for a major insurance company, and a former High School football coach. He and his wife have two adult children and two grandchildren. He enjoys spending time with his family, travel, golf, and is president of his church and sits on the synod council. Nick is grateful for his faith and the people in his life that believe in him. Nick has used his Attitude of Gratitude to get ahead in his career, and to develop strong relationships with his family, friends, and football players. Here is his story.

"I have always been one that if you told me I couldn't do something, I would take it as a challenge to prove you wrong. I'm not sure why, but that's just the way I am—and I'm okay with that!

When I was attending college, I worked for a men's clothing store as the youngest manager of the chain. One of my customers was a very successful agent with an insurance company. For a couple of months we had many conversations about what he did, and one day he asked if I would be open minded enough to look at an opportunity. My wife believed in me and finally convinced me I could do it if I really wanted to. Having someone who believes in me was a major influence on my decision! I had my first interview and they said that I might be too young for the job. I wasn't sure if they were testing me to see my reaction, or they really believed that I was too young. I since learned that no one gets an offer at that age in this large corporation. As I said, if you tell me I can't do something then I take it as a challenge to prove you wrong!

The manager I interviewed with was a member of the same church my family and I attended. He knew me there, but did not believe it was appropriate to recruit at church for his business. After a couple of interviews and meetings with the general manager of the office, and with approval from the home office, they offered me a position. I was grateful to the men who believed in me and I was determined not to let them down and to prove that they made the right decision.

This company had a "sales club" award convention every year based on production goals. I joined late in the year so they told me I could gear up for the next year. They felt it would be very hard to attain the sales club status in such a short time. That's all I needed to hear. I decided to bust my tail off and made the sales club, barely, but I did it! I proved them wrong—again!

As I look back at my life and experiences, I'm grateful to those who believed in me and helped me overcome all the challenges I've encountered. It reminds me what Chuck Swindoll says, "Life is 10% of what happens and 90% how you react to it!" Well, I've reacted with gratitude to those who believed in me, as well as other people who said I couldn't do something. After all, those other people gave me the motivation I needed—to prove them wrong!"

> *My reaction to anyone who tells me I can't do something is... prove them wrong!*
>
> —*Nick Cruz*

One Step at a Time

Suzanne is retired from public relations and enjoys spending time with her friends, two adult children, and grandchildren. She also enjoys travel, reading, scrapbooking, tending her roses, and her two dogs, Pixie and Biscuit. Suzanne managed to develop an Attitude of Gratitude while dealing with multiple challenges in her life. Here is her story.

"I heard the words come through the telephone, "They've found a large lesion on my brain." Time suddenly slowed to a crawl and a sense of other-worldliness took hold. My husband of 24 years was calling to tell me the outcome of his CAT scan. He didn't mind going alone to the hospital, he was confident—or perhaps in pre-denial. Is there such a thing?

For over 15 years, Bob suffered from severe migraines, hearing loss, ringing in the ear, and several other symptoms. Countless trips to family physicians and ear specialists offered a variety of possible causes, but no conclusive diagnosis. One night, sitting on the couch with me watching TV, he looked at me and said, "I wonder if I have a brain tumor?" A thread of fear began to weave itself into my heart. Denial pulled the thread. Brain tumors happen to other people—not to us. I refused to give in to hysteria. Long ago, I learned from my mother to face the dragon. When you've conquered "it", then you can fall apart.

Finally, the test results came back. I was so elated! It's not cancer! A call with the Doctor broke the tiny bubble of my hope. He said, "You must understand—this is a deadly brain tumor. It's the size of a goose egg or a man's fist, doubled up. It's putting extreme pressure on his brain stem and frankly, I'm surprised he is still alive." Wow.

Bob was an easy person to like and even to love, but unless he was center-stage, no one else mattered. I wasn't happy in my marriage. He was the master of passive-aggressive behavior. He took charge and I let him. Now the monster in his head was in charge of both of us.

The surgery would occur at a hospital better equipped to deal with such a massive tumor. Later on, they were to admit it was the largest brain tumor in that hospital's history. While talking to the doctors, my fairy tale world of denial turned into a clear, sharpened, defined reality. Every nuance, word, action, and activity took on real meaning to me. It would take two weeks to assemble the team (a massive grouping of neurosurgeons, nurses, anesthesiologists, et al), and the surgery would last over twenty hours.

On the day of the surgery, Bob is stoic. He wants to get it over. How little did he know, it was about to be over. Forever. No, he didn't die. But he did. What was left after 21 hours of surgery was a shell of the man he once was. The right side of his face was paralyzed which prevented legible speech and swallowing. His right arm and leg were weak and he needed a walker or wheelchair to get about. Before he was discharged a few months later, he suffered a moderate stroke and he required three more surgeries. At home, multiple therapies (speech, occupational, physical) strengthened what could be made stronger, but he would never be the same. It took me months to realize that his bright, strong, arrogant, bold, charismatic personality was sucked out of his life, along with the tumor.

Now I was in charge. No arrogance here. I didn't ask for this. I was the weakling. The girl raised by a "smother mother" who married a "control freak", I wanted to stay home, raise babies and cook Armenian food. I wasn't allowed to make decisions and frankly, I didn't want to!

I was overwhelmed. There were bills to be paid, children to minister to (kids, you are on your own now), and in-laws who moved in with us to care for their son during the day. We had a polite, but strained, and even sometimes-angry relationship. I had to tolerate them for nine months, but in the end, I felt a deep gratitude for their help. One step at a time; emotions to control and redirect, finances to settle and manage, a job to keep, long work hours, my own health to maintain, household to keep up with, and a family to hold together. One step at a time, that's all it takes—one step. The hardest part is the first footfall.

I quickly learned that reality is not an enemy; it is a challenging friend. It is an element that demands action that commands attention and seeks resolution—one step at a time. Reality won't go away, can't be wished away, and can never be escaped. Do you need perseverance? Meet reality. Patience? Meet Reality. Strength? Meet reality. Wisdom? Meet reality. One step at a time. Slowly, methodically, chipping away at each task, each need. Then there is the pause. A time to reflect. A time to look back. Compare this experience to driving up a mountain. You are aware of a slight incline as you progress further, but when you look back—not only do you see how far you've come, but how high.

My story doesn't end there. I had many trials during the 1990's, including my 80-year old father's death after a long illness, managing his long-term care, trust and financial matters, the death of my first grandchild, fear of losing my job, a legal battle over the estrangement from my second grandson, and finally, Bob's death after fourteen years of suffering. At one point, I jokingly told a friend that Danielle Steel was writing a novel about my life, and she believed me!

What have I learned from these challenges of life?

- Routines can be healing. A mundane activity, completed on a regular basis can bring a sense of control over the moment. I could not control the reality of a brain tumor. I can control when I brush my teeth or how I perform a task. Life may be "out of control," but it helps to control what you can.

- Find ways to soothe your soul and your senses. Pray, meditate, read spiritual literature or biographies of people who have survived great obstacles. I found I needed anything "soft" like a blanket, a pillow, or a sweater because the tactile "comfort" helped to soothe my senses.

- Don't just take "one day at a time," you may need to take one minute at a time. Learn to deal with the NOW. "Stressing out" over tomorrow's duties or obligations will only wear you out faster. Allow yourself to "take a break," even if it is only for five minutes. The refreshment can be amazing.

- When you are overwhelmed, a paper and pencil can be your therapist. Prioritize your life/actions/activities as much as you can

- Listen to your body. Sleep, eat well, try to exercise, and try to find a balance to the best of your ability. Don't rely on harmful substances to "get you through," relying on alcohol, tobacco, or drugs will only complicate your problems.

- Laugh! Yes, laugh as often as you can. Watch an old "Lucy" rerun; read a funny story or joke; spend time with friends who can make you chuckle; do anything that will allow you to find joy in life, once again. Try to put yourself in "normal" situations. You will find a sense of healing and strength to carry on, if you do.

Over twenty years have passed since Bob's surgery. I was able to continue working until retirement, and while I still struggle with vivid memories of those trying years, I have found a new strength and greater capacity to deal with multiple challenges, one step at a time!"

Do you need perseverance? Meet reality! Learn to deal with the NOW—one step at a time.

—*Suzanne Thomas*

Far Enough

John is a retired auto sales and service manager who lives with his wife and enjoys their three adult children and six grandchildren. He works part time as a blacksmith at an amusement park and he and his wife are active in their church. He volunteers at a local hospital visiting and comforting the patients and at a shelter for homeless men serving meals and handing out clothes. John has lived a long and fulfilling life. He came to the USA literally on a boat, but he hasn't gone far enough yet. Here is his story.

"My parents were farmers in Germany and raised my siblings and me to be hard working and thankful for what we had. Our family survived the Hitler years, keeping our family and farm intact. After completing my education, I trained as a blacksmith and then later on, I became a Volkswagen (VW) auto mechanic. The post-war years brought an economic decline and unemployment was at an all-time high. My uncle on my mother's side of the family was living in the United States so he agreed to be my sponsor and help me find work there. I didn't want to leave my family, but I said, "I've gone far enough." The promise of work led me to immigrate to another country.

I boarded a ship call the "Berlin" for the eleven-day journey to the USA. I had the time of my life on the ship. There was lots of excitement of new beginnings as we danced every night after dinner. The ship offloaded many people in Canada then set off to New York. As we passed the statue Liberty I was excited because knew I had arrived at my new home. I was optimistic and thankful for the opportunity to start a new life.

I was also a bit nervous because I didn't speak any English. Fortunately, I had German-speaking relatives who could help me get a job and learn the language. My aunt and uncle greeted me at the pier and took me to live with them at their home. My uncle helped me get into night school where I learned English three nights per week at a cost of a mere 25 cents. Then he took me to three VW dealers. Each one needed workers, but by the third one I said, "I've gone far enough." I found the place where I belonged and I am grateful to have worked there for seventeen years.

During this time, I met several girls who liked me, but as soon as I met my Wilma, again I said, "I've gone far enough." I found the woman I loved and we've been together ever since. I worked as a mechanic, then in the body shop as a welder. Wilma and I had two children and the boss promoted me to supervisor on the night shift. I worked at night and took over caring for our children in the afternoon so Wilma could get her rest. Wilma worked in a bakery on Saturdays and I would take the children out running errands with me. In those days men didn't take care of children, they thought it was a woman's job. That didn't bother me at all. I loved my wife and my children and I was grateful to have had that time with them when they were growing up.

I eventually worked my way up to become the service manager of the VW dealership. The general manager (GM) moved to Calgary, Alberta Canada where he bought his own dealership. He called and said, "Why don't you come and visit us here?" It was winter in New York and it was cold and snowy so it was not busy. I flew to Calgary and the GM gave me a grand tour of the area. It was clean and nice, and the snow was white. In contrast, New York was busy, the people weren't always nice, and the snow was a dirty brown. He took me to the mountains and after seeing all the people having fun skiing and the natural beauty of the whole area, I thought this was not too bad at all. I said, "I've gone far enough." I relocated my family to Calgary. I was thankful that the GM invited me to visit, although he was really recruiting me for his dealership. I worked at his dealership as the service manager, then salesman, and finally sales manager. I remained in the auto industry until I retired and I am grateful that it provided a good life for my family and me.

Wilma and I had another child and we enjoyed raising our son and two daughters in Canada. I am thankful all three have grown up and raised loving families of their own. They all found work they enjoy doing and are married to wonderful people. We love all of our six grandchildren; five girls and one boy (everyone teases him about being Wilma's favorite). Wilma and I are both grateful for our lives and the love we receive from our family.

As we grow older, we have our share of health issues. I've had both hips replaced and Wilma had one of her kidneys removed due to cancer. I was so nervous during her four-hour surgery and I'm grateful for the doctor who made sure the nurses updated me frequently. When it was finished, Wilma was in the recovery room and the nurses didn't allow me to see her for about two hours. Finally, they rolled her past me on the way to her hospital room. You have no idea how I felt to know she is alive! I thanked the doctor and the good Lord who made sure my Wilma would be with me forever.

I've lived a long and fulfilling life. I will always be thankful for those who gave me opportunity when I needed it and helped my family in sickness and health. I am grateful to have helped others in return when they needed it. I know at some time the good Lord will be giving me the most wonderful opportunity of all. When that time comes, I will know that I've gone, "Far enough."

I know when I've gone far enough!

—*John Claussen*

Reflect on Gratitude

Reflect on the following and discuss with ***Your People:***

1. Do I ever feel that I don't have enough time, money, or possessions?
2. What things do I have that I am thankful for, and why?
3. What good things have happened to me that I am grateful for, and why?
4. What bad things have happened to me that I am grateful for, and why?
5. How do I express my appreciation to other people?
6. How do I express my appreciation to myself?
7. What does "Pass it On" mean?
8. How do I Pass it On to other people?
9. Am I a Grateful Server, and in what ways?
10. In what ways do I provide Grateful Customer Service?
11. Do I lose sleep over problems? What am I doing about it?
12. Am I a Grateful Customer? In what ways?

REFLECT ON ATTITUDE

In his book *On Hiring*, recruiting expert Robert Half writes that, "You can infer a great deal about the attitudes and personality of the candidates through the way they answer questions." Keep this in mind as you reflect on attitude. Think about how someone interviewing you for a job may perceive the answers.

Reflect on the following and discuss with *Your People:*

1. What does Select Your Attitude mean?
2. What are my beliefs, values, and expectations about my family, friends, and co-workers?
3. What do the following statements mean to me?
   a. Our attitude creates a self-fulfilling prophecy: We become what we believe to be true.
   b. Everything you do is by choice.
   c. If you don't know what you do want, then move away from what you don't want.
   d. You're in the Possibility Zone when you overcome your Possibility Blockers by programming your mind to think differently.
   e. Motivation is a "want to" versus "have to" attitude.
   f. Pass it On means to give of yourself to others, without expecting anything in return.
4. How have I used my attitudes to accomplish my goals:
   a. Attitude of Choice?
   b. Attitude of Purpose?
   c. Attitude of Possibility?
   d. Attitude of Accountability?
   e. Attitude of Gratitude?
5. What opportunities for improvement do I have in selecting my attitude?

MANAGE YOUR GOALS	
1	**Manage Your Goals**
2	Set goals to achieve your purpose
3	Set smaller goals to achieve a larger goal
4	You must act on goals to achieve them
5	You can fulfill your purpose by managing goals
6	**Manage Goals With The Six P's**
7	Action words: Prepare, Plan, Perform, Prevail, Produce, Perfect
8	**Manage Your Resources**
9	Money, people, and possessions are renewable, time is not
10	Manage money; it pays for your goals
11	Manage people; seek out and nurture meaningful relationships
12	Manage possessions; take care of your things so they last

2. MANAGE YOUR GOALS

In the first chapter, we discussed how to Select Your Attitude and figure out a purpose in your personal and professional life. Now let's look at how to achieve it. Your purpose may be a slow journey over many years, not a destination reached quickly. It can be overwhelming to think about how to get there. As you manage goals, remember that it's not all about the destination. It's more about enjoying the journey along the way!

> *Life is a journey, not a destination.*
>
> —*Ralph Waldo Emerson*

GOAL MANAGEMENT. Goal management is the process of setting goals and tracking their progress until you achieve or change them.

> *Success is steady progress toward one's personal goals.*
>
> —*Jim Rohn*

PURPOSE. Successful people set goals for their journey even when they can't see the destination. Instead of one large lifetime goal, they set smaller goals to achieve their purpose.

> *Some people want it to happen, some wish it would happen, others make it happen.*
>
> —*Michael Jordan*

LARGE GOALS. Select an Attitude of Possibility and set large goals higher than you think possible. However, the thought of accomplishing a large goal can be overwhelming. If you can't see how to get from where you are to where you want to be, then think of smaller steps to get there.

> *I don't look to jump over 7-foot bars: I look around for 1-foot bars that I can step over.*
>
> —*Warren Buffett*

SMALL STEPS. Setting several smaller objectives will help achieve your larger goal over time. How do you eat a cow? Let me pause for a moment while you visualize the cow standing there, a fork and steak knife in hand, and a bib around the neck. So how do you do it? One steak at a time!

> Remember to dream big, think long-term, underachieve on a daily basis, and take baby steps. That is the key to long-term success.
>
> —Robert Kiyosaki

BHAG GOALS. It's much easier to set smaller goals than a "Big Hairy Audacious Goal" (BHAG, pronounced BEE-hag). James Collins and Jerry Porras describe it in their research book, *Built to Last: Successful Habits of Visionary Companies*. They describe a BHAG as a clear and compelling goal that may be risky and overwhelming, but creates excitement and motivation. You can achieve a BHAG by using S.M.I.L.E. to manage the smaller goals that lead up to it.

> Setting goals is the first step in turning the invisible into the visible.
>
> —Tony Robbins

GOALS REQUIRE ACTION. You must act on goals to achieve them. Be a Doer and manage goals for success!

> The most important key to achieving great success is to decide upon your goal and launch, get started, take action, move.
>
> —Brian Tracy

THE SIX P's OF MANAGING GOALS	
1	**Prepare**
2	Define your purpose, learn goal setting tools and techniques
3	**Plan**
4	Set goals with S.M.A.R.T. criteria
5	**Perform**
6	Implement goals, receive feedback, adjust or change
7	**Prevail**
8	S.M.I.L.E. and overcome obstacles and setbacks
9	**Produce**
10	Deliver the desired results and celebrate success!
11	**Perfect**
12	Continuous improvement, learn from success and failure

THE SIX P'S

The "Six P's" is an easy to remember method for managing goals. The method consists of action verbs: to prepare, to plan, to perform, to prevail, to produce, and to perfect goals.

The Six P's of managing goals is to:

1. PREPARE. Define your purpose, and learn goal management tools and techniques.

2. PLAN. S.M.A.R.T. goals: Specific, Measurable, Achievable, Relevant, and Time-bound.

3. PERFORM. Implement goals, receive feedback along the way, then adjust or change them.

4. PREVAIL. Overcome the obstacles and setbacks that may occur.

5. PRODUCE. Deliver the desired results and celebrate success.

6. PERFECT. Implement continuous improvement with lessons learned from both success and failure.

Prepare

There are several things to do before setting goals. The following preparations will help make the process easier, more effective, and much more enjoyable.

> *By failing to prepare, you are preparing to fail.*
> —*Benjamin Franklin*

BE A PROJECTILE, NOT A PINBALL. Avoid what I call the "Pinball Path." A pinball starts on its path with a push from a plunger. The flippers hit the ball and it randomly bounces off obstacles in the pinball machine. A pinball has no goals, so someone else determines its path. On the other hand, a projectile is like a missile; rocket propelled with an internal guidance system. A missile knows where it's going and almost nothing can stop it from hitting the target. Select an Attitude of Purpose and be a projectile, not a pinball!

> *I'm not a ball in a pinball machine. I know what I want.*
> —*Emile Hirsch*

CHOOSE YOUR SUCCESS. Success starts by deciding what you want. Select an Attitude of Possibility and aim high!

> *The indispensable first step to getting the things you want out of life is this: decide what you want.*
> —*Ben Stein*

ASK WHY? "Why do I want to be successful? Is it for accomplishment, challenge, meaning, relationships, wealth, or something else?

> *Being the richest man in the cemetery doesn't matter to me. Going to bed at night saying we've done something wonderful, that's what matters to me.*
> —*Steve Jobs*

ASK WHY NOT? "Why not, what's the worst thing that could happen?" Don't be overly risk-averse. The higher the risk, the bigger the reward!

> *Bad things are not the worst things that can happen to us. Nothing is the worst thing that can happen to us!*
> —*Richard Bach*

ASK WHAT? "What are the results I want?" Do I want happiness, joy, peace, satisfaction, or something else?

> *Success is getting what you want; happiness is wanting what you get.*
>
> —*Ingrid Bergman*

PURPOSE AND VALUE. "What is the purpose and value of my goal?" Why is my goal important to me (the purpose)? Why is it important to others (the value)?

> *Strive not to be a success, but rather to be of value.*
>
> —*Albert Einstein*

START SMALL. You don't have to be the best at anything, nor change the world to be successful.

> *Not all of us can do great things. But we can do small things with great love.*
>
> —*Mother Teresa*

AIM HIGH. If perfection is the goal, then excellence is acceptable, and average is hitting the mark. Don't be just average, be excellent!

> *We aim above the mark to hit the mark.*
>
> —*Ralph Waldo Emerson*

DOER NOT DREAMER. Success requires changing wants into goals. Goals achieve purpose in life. Use S.M.I.L.E. to set goals and achieve your purpose!

> *Goals are dreams with deadlines.*
>
> —*Diana Scharf Hunt*

TO PREPARE SUMMARY. Select an Attitude of Purpose and involve **Your People** to help figure out what you want in life.

> *Destiny is not a matter of chance, it is a matter of choice. It is not a thing to be waited for, it is a thing to be achieved.*
> —*William Jennings Bryan*

Plan

It takes planning to complete goals successfully. They may be small objectives, several large goals, or a plan for the rest of your life. Decide what you want to do or become, then set goals to achieve it.

> *Only those who will risk going too far can possibly find out how far one can go.*
>
> —*T.S. Eliot*

YOUR PLAN. If there is no plan then someone else will make one for you. By making a plan and accepting responsibility for the outcome, you'll create the motivation from within for success.

> *If you don't design your own life plan, chances are you'll fall into someone else's plan. And guess what they have planned for you? Not much.*
>
> —*Jim Rohn*

TOOLS AND TECHNIQUES. Learn and use goal management tools and techniques to effectively set and manage goals for success. School and organizations may have training programs for low or no cost. **Your People** can help turn that training into action.

> *The secret to productive goal setting is in establishing clearly defined goals, writing them down and then focusing on them several times a day with words, pictures and emotions as if we've already achieved them.*
>
> —*Denis Waitley*

GOAL CRITERIA. Commonly attributed to Drucker and Doran, S.M.A.R.T. goals are Specific, Measurable, Achievable, Relevant, and Time-bound.

> *It is the combination of the objective and its action plan that is really important.*
>
> —*George T. Donan*

GOAL SHEET	
	GOAL SHEET
1	**Purpose of a Goal Sheet**
2	Track progress against the criteria you set
3	Use a goal sheet for both goals and smaller objectives
4	**Written as Affirmations**
5	In the present tense as if you have already achieved the goal
6	The RAS will kick in and help focus on what you need
7	**Write Down Your Goals And Review Them Often**
8	S.M.A.R.T. criteria used on the goal sheet:
9	Specific, Measurable, Achievable, Realistic, Time-bound
10	**Involve Your People**
11	Select an Attitude of Accountability
12	Involve *Your People* to plan goals that will achieve your purpose

GOAL SHEET. The most effective goals are those written down and reviewed often. By reviewing goals, you'll be able to see progress, anticipate changes needed to keep on track, and sustain motivation for success. There is an example of a goal sheet in the Appendix. At the top of the sheet are the column headers. Each column is a letter from the S.M.A.R.T. acronym. Enter the goal on a row from left to right, specifying each of the criteria. The example is brief by design but you can customize it as needed to help achieve goals.

> *Without continual growth and progress, such words as improvement, achievement, and success have no meaning.*
> —Benjamin Franklin

WRITTEN AS AFFIRMATIONS. Write down goals as positive affirmations. Reading and affirming goals will convince the subconscious that you've already achieved them. The subconscious will strive for sanity by kicking in the RAS and help focus on what you need to complete goals.

> *By recording your dreams and goals on paper, you set in motion the process of becoming the person you most want to be.*
> —Mark Victor Hansen

KEY POINTS. The key points of planning goals are:

1. SPECIFIC
    a. Clear and unambiguous.
    b. Answer the five W's: Who, What, When, Where, Why?
2. MEASURABLE
    a. Objective criteria (facts), versus subjective (opinions).
    b. How many, how long, what standards for quality?
3. ACHIEVABLE
    a. Realistic and attainable.
    b. Is it achievable within the timeframe specified?
4. RELEVANT
    a. Goals that matter to you and others.
    b. Do I really need this?
5. TIME-BOUND
    a. Target milestones and dates for completion.
    b. What is the schedule and due date?

TO PLAN SUMMARY. Select an Attitude of Accountability and involve **Your People** to plan goals that will achieve your purpose.

> *Crystallize your goals. Make a plan for achieving them and set yourself a deadline. Then, with supreme confidence, determination and disregard for obstacles and other people's criticisms, carry out your plan.*
>
> —*Paul J. Meyer*

Perform

Now that you have a purpose and goals, it's time to take action. The first step of performing goals is to select all of your attitudes for success; choice, purpose, possibility, accountability, and gratitude. Be responsible for choices, empowered to take action, and accountable for the results. Get started today and create the inner motivation needed to perform goals and prevail on the path to success!

Know your goal, make a plan and pull the trigger.
—*Phil C. McGraw*

FEEDBACK IS ESSENTIAL. The letter "M" in S.M.A.R.T. criteria is "Measurable." Feedback is essential to measure the progress of goals. It's an opportunity to adjust or change a failing goal, before it's too late. With all your efforts to achieve goals, make sure to build in time for feedback. It can be an informal check-in, or a formal sit down and discussion. **Your People** will give constructive criticism, encouragement, and recognition needed to achieve goals.

Review your goals twice every day in order to be focused on achieving them.
—*Les Brown*

REEVALUATE AND ADJUST. Reevaluate goals often to determine if they're still going to achieve the desired result. Situations and priorities may change over time. Accept Change, adapt with it, and adjust goals as necessary to stay on track.

Goals allow you to control the direction of change in your favor.
—*Brian Tracy*

DON'T FLATTEN OUT. Have you ever felt "flat" after achieving a goal? Most of us have. It's not that the goal wasn't important; it's just how we are. According to Aristotle, it's our teleological nature, meaning the need to set and achieve goals. Feeling "flat" is our way of knowing when it's time to set a new goal. Avoid flattening out by setting the next goal before finishing the current one.

Arriving at one goal is the starting point to another.
—*John Dewey*

TO PERFORM SUMMARY. Select an Attitude of Purpose and involve **Your People** to perform the action necessary to achieve your goals.

> *A desire presupposes the possibility of action to achieve it; action presupposes a goal which is worth achieving.*
>
> —*Ayn Rand*

Prevail

As the saying goes, "Anything that can happen will happen!" An Attitude of Possibility assures us that "anything" includes success! We've all experienced changes, obstacles, and setbacks. How we respond can often make the difference whether or not we achieve goals.

> *It had long since come to my attention that people of accomplishment rarely sat back and let things happen to them. They went out and happened to things.*
>
> —*Leonardo da Vinci*

EXPECT THE UNEXPECTED. Plan for what I call the "Toyota Principle". During the 1970s, Toyota launched one of its most memorable marketing campaigns with the jingle "You asked for it, you got it!" The Toyota Principle is from an old adage that warns us to, "Be careful what you ask for because you may get it!" In other words, be careful to set the right goals for the expected results, and be open to an unexpected outcome.

> *To expect the unexpected shows a thoroughly modern intellect.*
>
> —*Oscar Wilde*

EXPECT SETBACKS. Setbacks are going to happen. Respond, don't just react. Turn setbacks into unexpected results!

> *If you so choose, even the unexpected setbacks can bring new and positive possibilities. If you so choose, you can find value and fulfillment in every circumstance.*
>
> —*Ralph Marston*

OVERCOME SETBACKS. Remain in the Possibility Zone to prevail over adversity. Visualization and affirmations are powerful methods to stay in the zone. For example, "I feel a sense of accomplishment every time I prevail over a setback!" Affirm this to yourself often, and don't forget to celebrate the success of overcoming setbacks.

> *Life is a series of experiences, each one of which makes us bigger, even though sometimes it is hard to realize this. For the world was built to develop character, and we must learn that the setbacks and grieves which we endure help us in our marching onward.*
>
> *—Henry Ford*

TO PREVAIL SUMMARY. Select an Attitude of Accountability and use resilience to prevail over setbacks. Plan for the best, prepare for the worst, and prevail over adversity.

> *Expect the best. Prepare for the worst. Capitalize on what comes.*
>
> *—Zig Ziglar*

Produce

Goal setting is necessary for success, and managing goals with feedback is essential. But in the end, you must achieve or produce something. Whether it's for another or yourself, you are accountable to produce a successful outcome or a profitable result. Success depends on the ability to communicate what the goal was, what you did to achieve it, and what the results were. Reporting the results is crucial for success, and for those who helped produce them.

> *However beautiful the strategy, you should occasionally look at the results.*
>
> *—Winston Churchill*

RESULTS. A concise status report is an excellent way to keep the boss informed. There is an example of a status report in the Appendix. The boss won't be able to give the priority needed in their problem queue unless you clearly show why the goal requires more resources, and a place higher in the queue. In addition, they won't give the team recognition for a job well done, unless they know what they did to deserve it. Reporting results is not boastful or selfish; it's necessary for success.

Admit it: you hate writing a status report for your manager every week. Every manager has a different format for writing it, it seems no one looks at it, and every manager wants something different on it. Did I mention it is a pain to write? All true. I'd contend, however, that the lowly status report—written correctly—is your ultimate communications tool to show your results from your work.

—Scot Herrick

ACCOUNTABILITY. Make the choices necessary to achieve or produce results. Be accountable for choices. Don't think of consequences as punishment. Think of them as rewards for a job well done when things go well, or learnings for the future if they don't.

Perhaps his might be one of the natures where a wise estimate of consequences is fused in the fires of that passionate belief which determines the consequences it believes in.

—George Eliot

CELEBRATE RESULTS. Celebrate success to motivate others and yourself.

The more you praise and celebrate your life, the more there is in life to celebrate.

—Oprah Winfrey

HAVE SOME FUN. Loosen up and enjoy the celebration; you earned it!

Celebrate your success and find humor in your failures. Don't take yourself so seriously. Loosen up and everyone around you will loosen up. Have fun and always show enthusiasm.

—Sam Walton

TO PRODUCE SUMMARY. Produce or achieve goals, be accountable for the results, and celebrate success with the people who helped along the way.

The major reason for setting a goal is for what it makes of you to accomplish it. What it makes of you will always be the far greater value than what you get.

—Jim Rohn

Perfect

We prepared our purpose, planned a goal, and performed it. Then we set the next one, prevailed over setbacks, and produced a report of the results. Finally, we celebrated success. Now it's time to look back at what happened, and think about what we can do better the next time. Statistician Dr. W. Edwards Deming describes the concept of continuous improvement in his groundbreaking book, *Out of the Crisis.* Deming teaches us to improve processes by analyzing lessons learned from both failure and success. The objective is to produce what Toyota manufacturing expert Shigeo Shingo calls in his book, *Key Strategies for Plant Improvement,* an "easier, better, faster and cheaper" result.

> *It is not enough to do your best; you must know what to do, and then do your best.*
>
> —*W. Edwards Deming*

PERFECTION. We've all heard the expression, "Perfection is the goal." Many people fail because they set standards of perfection that are unrealistic and unattainable. It's motivating to aspire for it, but expecting perfection from ourselves, or others, can only lead to disappointment and regret.

> *If a man should happen to reach perfection in this world, he would have to die immediately to enjoy himself.*
>
> —*Josh Billings*

PERFECTIONISM. If left unchecked, perfectionism can lead to a self-defeating prophecy: "I failed therefore I am the worst, I do not deserve a happy family or job, and I cannot forgive myself or other people." Ask **Your People** to help set personal standards that are realistic and attainable. This can lead to a self-affirming prophecy: "I learn from failures to become my best, I deserve a happy family and job, and I have compassion for myself and other people."

> *Better to do something imperfectly than to do nothing flawlessly.*
>
> —*Robert H. Schuller*

SETUP FOR SUCCESS. Set yourself up for success by aiming for perfection, but acknowledge the fact that being flawless is unattainable. Strive to be the best you can be with continuous improvement. What do you call the two medical school graduates from the same class, and with the highest and the lowest grade point average? You call both of them "Doctor!"

> *Perfection is not attainable, but if we chase perfection we can catch excellence.*
>
> —*Vince Lombardi*

KEY POINTS. The key points of perfecting goals with continuous improvement are:

1. Reflect on the results.
   a. Did I become or produce what I set my goal to achieve?
   b. Does the result align with my purpose?
2. Reflect on performance by asking, "How did I do at…"
   a. …Selecting my attitude?
   b. …Managing my goals?
   c. …Investing in myself?
   d. …Living a balanced life?
   e. …Embracing change?
3. Reflect on start, stop, and continue.
   a. What I should start to do next time that I didn't do the last time?
   b. What wasn't effective that I should stop doing?
   c. What was effective that I should continue?
4. Set goals for continuous improvement.
   a. Use answers to the reflections above to set future goals.
   b. S.M.I.L.E. and set goals for continuous improvement.

TO PERFECT SUMMARY. Involve **Your People** and others to reflect on how to use continuous improvement to achieve future goals.

> *If there was nothing wrong in the world there wouldn't be anything for us to do.*
>
> —*George Bernard Shaw*

MANAGE YOUR RESOURCES

The previous section was on managing goals to achieve your purpose. To accomplish goals, you'll need to acquire and manage resources, including time, money, people, and possessions.

> *Great emergencies and crises show us how much greater our vital resources are than we had supposed.*
>
> —*William James*

DON'T WAIT. In his book, *Goal Setting 101: How to Set and Achieve a Goal,* goal management expert Gary Ryan Blair advises that rarely will there be all the resources needed to accomplish goals. In most cases, there simply aren't enough, and you have to start before completely ready. This is where the expression "ready, fire, aim" comes from. To hit a target, you normally get the weapon ready, aim at the center, then fire. Often there isn't enough time to aim; but if you wait to fire, the opportunity to hit the target is lost. If all resources aren't available, then get ready and fire before being completely satisfied with your aim.

> *You cannot afford to wait for perfect conditions. Goal setting is often a matter of balancing timing against available resources. Opportunities are easily lost while waiting for perfect conditions.*
>
> —*Gary Ryan Blair*

MANAGE YOUR TIME. The most valuable resource is time. Frequently ask, "What's the best use of my time right now?"

> *In all planning you make a list and you set priorities. Review our priorities, ask the question; what's the best use of our time right now?*
>
> —*Alan Lakein*

TIME ISN'T RENEWABLE. Money, people, and possessions are renewable resources. Time is not. Your time is precious, limited, and irreplaceable. Use it well.

> *Time is the coin of your life. It is the only coin you have, and only you can determine how it will be spent. Be careful lest you let other people spend it for you.*
>
> —*Carl Sandburg*

MANAGE YOUR MONEY. Financial goals pay for most life goals. Adapt your financial goals as life goals change. Successful people tend to set financial goals higher than they think possible.

> *It takes courage to stretch your limits, express your power, and fulfill your potential... it's no different in the financial realm.*
>
> —*Suze Orman*

MONEY AND GOALS. Money is required to achieve many goals. Make financial plans to fund them. You cannot achieve some goals if there is not enough money to pay for them.

> *If you're interested in becoming successful in a material sense, you've got to be able to handle financial pressure. By that I mean knowing how to give, receive, earn, spend, and save.*
>
> —*Lou Tice*

MANAGE YOUR PEOPLE. Seek out and nurture meaningful relationships. Some may be one-way relationships helping other people. Others may be two-way relationships caring and supporting each other. Consider what kind of relationship you have with other people. If it's not a healthy relationship, then it may not be worth continuing. Otherwise, nurture a healthy relationship to keep it meaningful.

> *You must constantly ask yourself these questions: Who am I around? What are they doing to me? What have they got me reading? What have they got me saying? Where do they have me going? What do they have me thinking? And most important, what do they have me becoming? Then ask yourself the big question: Is that okay? Your life does not get better by chance, it gets better by change.*
>
> —*Jim Rohn*

MANAGE YOUR POSSESSIONS. Take care of things you own so they'll last longer and return the full value of their cost. Reduce stress and live a more balanced life by managing your possessions.

> *Unnecessary possessions are unnecessary burdens. If you have them, you have to take care of them! There is great freedom in simplicity of living. It is those who have enough but not too much who are the happiest.*
>
> —*Peace Pilgrim*

STORIES ON GOALS

The following stories are on this chapter, *Manage Your Goals*:

- Get Started
- How Hard Can it Be?
- Goal Setting Works

Get Started

When I was 17, my parents asked me "the question." You know the one. It goes like this: "What are you going to do with your life?" Heck, I didn't know. I had no idea. I was about to graduate High School, but I didn't have a passion for anything. Yes, I was a straight-A student, but with no motivation for college. Sure, I had a few hobbies and part-time jobs, but no burning desire to make any of them a career.

After a few discussions with my college counselor and my parents, I was so confused that I just gave up. I'm not sure what language the counselor was speaking, but I couldn't understand it. My parents didn't go to college so I think it was just as confusing to them. I figured out that college requires money, but I didn't figure out how to pay for it. My head hurt.

Playing the trumpet was fun and I was good at it. However, few rock bands had horns and the symphony was boring to me at the time. I taught myself how to play the guitar, but without a singing voice, I was never going to be a rock star. My heart sank.

Taking electronic things apart and putting them back together was enjoying to me. One time I tore down a record player and re-purposed

105

the record needle as a guitar pickup. Then I re-wired the amplifier so I could turn my acoustic into an electric guitar. Crude, yes, but it worked. However, I didn't know how to turn this hobby into a job. Alas, my spirit was broken.

You can imagine how unhappy I was. At the time, I felt like my parents were kicking me out of the house, but I'm sure they were just trying to help get my life started. It was very stressful and discouraging. As I describe in the section *Stories on Purpose*, some interesting things happened that led me to join the Army. I decided to turn my electronics hobby into a real job so I could make enough money to pay for college.

The clouds parted, the birds sang, and the sun came out again. Wow, I felt like a ton of bricks suddenly lifted off my shoulders. My head stopped hurting, my heart was full, and my spirit was soaring high. I had ambition, plans, and the most important thing I needed. You see, now I had a goal!

Regardless of age or circumstance, you can do or become whatever you choose. Get started by using S.M.I.L.E. to set a goal. It changed my life and I know it can also change yours!

How Hard Can it Be?

I've used cell phones for many years, starting with the famous Motorola "brick". A few years ago, I decided to upgrade from a cell phone to a smartphone. I wanted the newly introduced Apple iPhone, but it was only available from one carrier who had the poorest reception in my area. Therefore, I decided to wait until the iPhone was available from my carrier who had better reception.

At the same time, my friend published *The Piano Chord Book You Can Actually Use!* It's a great reference guide on piano chord structures, and it includes pictures how to position your fingers on the keyboard for each chord. He gave me an advanced copy for review and I mentioned this would be a great app on a smartphone.

We both thought it would be a "cool" hobby with no expectation of commercial success. We agreed that he would create the graphic artwork and sounds. I had computer programming experience so I would create the smartphone app.

Soon thereafter, a line of smartphones based on the new Android operating system exploded on the market. The iPhone was not going to be available on my carrier for another year so I made the decision to go with Android. My friend and I figured we would test our app in the new Android market, versus trying to compete with similar apps in the iStore. I purchased my Android, took two weeks off work, and began developing the app. My thinking was, "How hard can it be?"

No problem, I'll just learn how to program in the Android operating system, how to display the pictures, play the sound, and handle the finger swipes on the phone display. Oh, and I'll have to learn how to publish and market the app, as well as how to include advertisements. Okay, that's about three years of learning in just two weeks. I was beginning to see just how hard it could be!

It took much more than two weeks, and the hardest part was the time commitment. My fulltime job and business travel required more than forty hours per week. My friend and I knew we had to get our app published as soon as possible. We wanted to be the first to publish this type of app in the new Android market. I faced many technical challenges and had to re-design the app several times. We finally published it and enjoyed seeing our work well received around the world.

Over the next several months, I self-published several other Android apps, but this hobby was taking too much time. I knew I had lost my work/life/hobby balance, so I exited the market. After a couple of major updates to *The Piano Chord Book* app, I wasn't able to devote any more time so I handed everything over to my friend. Our app didn't go viral and we didn't make a fortune, but we did become "thousandaires." You can still find his book and instructional videos online.

I set a goal, persevered, and achieved it. I consider it a significant accomplishment in my life. In some situations, it's a great way to start a conversation and people enjoy meeting someone who has actually published an app. It's fun to display a slide of my apps at public speaking engagements, and it looks "cool" on my résumé.

I had an idea, developed a passion, set a goal, used all my resources, invested in my learning, published the app, and celebrated my success. And the most important, I rebalanced my life afterwards. I encourage you to dream about what you want and set goals to achieve it. After all, "How hard can it be?"

Goal Setting Works

Have you set a goal for everything achieved in life? I certainly haven't. I started setting goals only after attending an *Investment in Excellence*® course by The Pacific Institute. Its founder, the late Lou Tice, presented all the material via video lessons. Lou was an incredibly gifted speaker who inspired me to start setting goals. Now I plan my life the way I want to live it. Thank you, Lou!

During my career as a computer technician, I realized that my position could offer only so much in terms of challenge and compensation. I finally decided to become a manager, and that required me to pass a management review board. When I learned I had to sit alone in front of several seasoned managers, and they would rapid-fire questions about anything and everything at me, I found myself in my Uncomfortable Zone.

I was so ambitious that I loved being there. One of my soon-to-be peers unselfishly spent many day, nights, and weekends to help me prepare for the board. I wrote down my S.M.A.R.T. goals, and I used all the S.M.I.L.E. tools in the Possibility Zone: affirmations, self-talk, visualization, and Positive Wizards. Sure, I was a bit nervous when I first got there, but it soon faded away as I realized my preparation was paying off. I am proud to have passed the board on my first attempt. After putting this entire goal setting "stuff" into practice, I knew it worked so I was ready for many more goals ahead.

After a few management positions, I decided that a senior management position didn't offer the work/life balance I wanted for family and myself. Mentoring and professional networking paid off when I was offered a position as a Project Manager. Subsequently, I learned about the "Project Management Professional", or "PMP®", certification program by the Project Management Institute. I hand wrote the letters "PMP®" on my business card, kept it on my desk, and visualized my success on future challenging projects.

Again, I wrote down my goals, used all the S.M.I.L.E. tools, and prepared for the certification exam. To say the exam was a challenge is an understatement, big-time. It had a very low pass rate not only for the first try, but also for the second and third attempts. I was scared and very deep in my Uncomfortable Zone!

I took courses, studied, and started taking the practice exams. This was a two-year process and I was only five days from the exam date. I was failing every practice exam, even though I'd taken them many times. I used my Attitude of Possibility and kicked it into high gear by convincing my manager to give me the week off for training. That way I could focus on the exam with no distractions from work. Finally, only two days before the exam, I started passing the practice exams. Whew!

The only way to pass the exam is to memorize many different things, including one double-sided page of mathematical formulas. Critical path, earned value, net present value, you name it and it was on the sheet. I developed a mnemonic system to memorize both sides and I practiced recalling it repeatedly.

The exam was at a commercial testing facility with a proctor carefully monitoring every move I made. He said to start and to his amazement, I didn't even look at the test. I took out a piece of paper and wrote down formulas on both sides. All of them. He was getting nervous because it was a timed test, about 10 minutes had elapsed, and I hadn't even started the test yet! I was so in focus with my Attitude of Purpose that nothing could distract me. I achieved my goal by passing the test, and then I celebrated success with "*My People*".

The experiences of becoming a manager and achieving my project management certification were very memorable and rewarding. Both experiences, as well as others, have helped me set and achieve many personal and professional goals over the years.

I've experienced challenges and obstacles along the way, and I've recovered from some setbacks more gracefully than other ones. In the end, I've proven to myself that S.M.I.L.E. goal setting works. After all, you're reading another one of my goals right now!

REFLECT ON GOALS

Reflect on the following and discuss with *Your People:*

1. What does "life is a journey not a destination" mean?
2. How do my goals relate to my purpose in life?
3. What is a "Big Hairy Audacious Goal?"
4. What if I can't see how to achieve a large goal?
5. What is goal management?
6. Can I describe each of the Six P's?
7. How can I use each of the Six P's to achieve my goals?
8. What is the most important step of the Six P's and why?
9. Can I describe each of the S.M.A.R.T criteria?
10. Why should I write my goal sheets as affirmations in the present tense?
11. Why do I feel "flat" after achieving a goal?
12. What can I do to prevent feeling "flat" in the future?
13. What is the "Toyota Principle?"
14. Do I plan for the best, prepare for the worst, and prevail over adversity?
15. Do I celebrate results after I achieve a goal?
16. In what ways do I loosen up and have some fun after achieving a goal?
17. Does my perfectionism create a self-defeating prophecy for my life?
18. What does "set yourself up for success" mean?
19. What are the steps for continuous improvement and do I use them?
20. What are my resources, and in what ways do I manage them to achieve my goals?

INVEST IN YOURSELF	
1	**Appearance Matters**
2	It shouldn't matter, but it does
3	Do the right thing to make an appropriate impression on others
4	**Education and Training**
5	Learn the knowledge and skills needed to achieve goals
6	Manage goals for education and training
7	**Added Value Support**
8	Anticipate needs, ask effective questions, deliver on the promise
9	No surprises, do more than is expected
10	"What can I do right now that is more than expected of me?"
11	**Know your Elevator Pitch**
12	A valuable skill that will differentiate you from others

3. INVEST IN YOURSELF

The first two chapters were on how to Select Your Attitude and manage goals for success. This chapter is on the ways to invest in yourself with appearance, education and training, an elevator pitch, and what I call "Added Value Support".

One way to invest in yourself is with personal development. One of America's foremost business philosophers and experts on personal development is Jim Rohn. In his best-selling book, *The Five Major Pieces to the Life Puzzle*, he writes that we attract success by increasing value through personal development.

> *Success must be attracted, not pursued … Better results come from being a better person.*
>
> —*Jim Rohn*

IT PAYS. It's sensible, not selfish to invest in yourself.

> *An investment in knowledge pays the best interest.*
>
> —*Benjamin Franklin*

CHOOSE SUCCESS. Choose to be successful because the other options are mediocrity or failure.

> *Be miserable. Or motivate yourself. Whatever has to be done, it's always your choice.*
>
> —*Wayne Dyer*

DON'T GO IT ALONE. No one expects you to become successful on your own. Don't be afraid to ask for help.

> *You are never strong enough that you don't need help.*
>
> —*Cesar Chavez*

INVOLVE YOUR PEOPLE. Define what success is for yourself, and achieve it with the help of others.

> No one who achieves success does so without acknowledging the help of others. The wise and confident acknowledge this help with gratitude.
>
> — Alfred North Whitehead

GIVE YOURSELF PERMISSION. It's okay to seek out **Your People**. They actually want you to!

APPEARANCE MATTERS

Our appearance shouldn't matter, but it does. Other people constantly judge our appearance and behavior. We make an impression on others whether we care about what they think or not. We have the opportunity to make a positive impression on people we meet. Appearance is a choice and often influences how other people treat us.

Appearance in our politically correct world is a touchy subject. Regardless, we should always do the right thing when it comes to appearance—what we project to others, and what we perceive about them. Listen to what **Your People** say about appearance, and respond by making the changes necessary for success.

> Behavior is the mirror in which everyone shows their image.
> — Johann Wolfgang von Goethe

KEY POINTS. The key points of appearance are:

- BEHAVIOR. You don't always have to be on your best behavior. That would be boring. There is nothing wrong with having some fun and acting out, as long as you're not offending others or breaking laws. However, it is wrong to behave the way you want to rather than what is appropriate. Choose accordingly.

- GROOMING. You don't have to go to extremes—just clean, appropriate, and not offensive to others. Choose grooming that makes you feel good, and makes others feel good about you.

- RIGHT TIME AND PLACE. Appearance might be hindering your success. There is a right time and place. Choose behavior and grooming that is appropriate to the situation. Choose wisely.

EDUCATION AND TRAINING

S.M.I.L.E. offers many keys to success. Unlock your full potential with investments in education and training.

> *Learn everything you can, anytime you can, from anyone you can—there will always come a time when you will be grateful you did.*
>
> —*Sarah Caldwell*

CONTINUOUS DEVELOPMENT. Education can be formal or informal. Formal education is gaining knowledge, typically from a school. Informal education is self-study from people, books, and recorded media. Training is gaining a skill for a hobby or a job, typically from a coach or trade school. You achieve success by setting goals for education and training, regardless of age and experience. Continue education and training throughout your life. Knowledge and skills may be needed for a future goal you haven't even thought about yet.

> *The object of education is to prepare the young to educate themselves throughout their lives.*
>
> —*Robert M. Hutchins*

GOALS FOR DEVELOPMENT. The knowledge and skills required to achieve goals will determine how much education and training you need. Include education and training in goal planning. Invest in Yourself for success!

> *The principle goal of education in the schools should be creating men and women who are capable of doing new things, not simply repeating what other generations have done*
>
> —*Jean Piaget*

KEY POINTS. Education and training will help your personal development in the following areas. There are tips on creative thinking, time management, and organization in the Appendix, under self-management tips.

- COMMUNICATION. Writing, speaking, listening, presenting.
- COMPUTER. Typing, browser, email, multi-media, office suite.
- CREATIVE. Art, dance, design, music, performance, photography.
- FINANCE. Basic level of accounting, estimates, mental math.
- LEADERSHIP. Leading teams, supervision, management.
- ORGANIZATION AND TIME MANAGEMENT. Electronic media, paper, scheduling.
- PEOPLE. Critical thinking, interpersonal and social skills, relationship building.
- SALES AND MARKETING. Advertising, prospecting, selling and closing the deal.
- SOFT SKILLS. Critical thinking, influence, negotiation, persuasion, problem solving, teamwork.
- STRESS MANAGEMENT. Diet, exercise, fun, relaxation.

ADDED VALUE SUPPORT	
1	**Anticipate Needs**
2	Ask questions from their perspective: think, feel, want, need, act
3	**Ask Effective Questions**
4	Explain why you're asking, get to the point, and don't ramble
5	**Deliver on the Promise**
6	Set expectations in advance, then deliver
7	**No Surprises**
8	Reset expectations if necessary—before the deadline
9	**Do More Than is Expected**
10	Do what is wanted, anticipate what is needed, and deliver both
11	**Invest in Yourself by providing Added Value Support to Others**
12	"What can I do right now that is more than expected of me?"

Added Value Support

When assigned a task, do you just do what is necessary, or do you go "above and beyond?" "Added Value Support" is delivering more than is expected. The value given to others is an investment in yourself. It pays dividends in the satisfaction of serving others, recognition of accomplishment, and advancement opportunities. Give Added Value Support and accelerate your path to success!

Tony Jeary, known as *The RESULTS Guy*^{TM}, is a coach to the world's top CEOs. His signature book, *Strategic Acceleration: Succeed at the Speed of Life*, summarizes all of his strategic principles as the relationship of value to results. Tony agrees that personal development increases value, and improves results.

> *Give value. Do more than is expected.*
>
> — *Tony Jeary*

WHAT CAN I DO? Invest in yourself by giving Added Value Support to others. Frequently ask yourself "What can I do right now that is more than expected of me?"

> *The value of a man should be seen in what he gives and not in what he is able to receive.*
>
> — *Albert Einstein*

KEY POINTS. The key points of Added Value Support are:

- ANTICIPATE NEEDS. Ask questions from the other person's perspective: think, feel, want, need, and act.
- ASK EFFECTIVE QUESTIONS. Explain why you're asking, get to the point, and don't ramble. Depending on the situation, ask open or closed-ended questions.
- DELIVER ON THE PROMISE. Set their expectations before accepting the task, then deliver accurate and timely results
- NO SURPRISES. If necessary, reset expectations before the deadline.
- DO MORE THAN IS EXPECTED. Do what they want, anticipate what they really need, and deliver both.

Anticipate Needs

You've probably heard the expression "put yourself in their shoes." It means to think of the problem or situation from another person's point of view. Start by getting to know them. Then ask yourself questions on what they may think, feel, want, and need. Next, think about how they would act in the same situation. Finally, it takes empathy and self-esteem to accommodate the needs of others without letting them take advantage of you. Invest in Yourself by anticipating the needs of others.

> *Think as you work, for in the final analysis, your worth to your company comes not only in solving problems, but also in anticipating them.*
>
> —*Tom Lehrer*

Ask Effective Questions

How do you know what other people need? You ask them! However, they won't explain what they need unless you ask the right questions in the right way. Added Value Support is exceeding the expectations of others, and it starts by asking effective questions.

> *Successful people ask better questions, and as a result, they get better answers.*
>
> —*Tony Robbins*

TYPES OF QUESTIONS. There are many types of questions: convergent or closed-ended, divergent or open-ended, evaluative, factual, hypothetical, leading, multiple, probing, rhetorical, trick questions, or combinations of all types. Use the types of questions that match the information and level of detail needed. There are many types of questions to ask and many different ways to ask them. Whichever types of questions you ask, make sure they are effective ones!

> *Sometimes questions are more important than answers.*
>
> —*Nancy Willard*

OPEN AND CLOSED. Two of the most common types of questions are open-ended and closed-ended. The key differences are as follows.

OPEN-ENDED. An open-ended question has no specific answer. The advantage of an open-ended question is the quality of the information received. You get the answer as well as a detailed explanation. People will share their ideas, creativity, and feelings. The disadvantage of an open-ended question is that the person could ramble on and dominate the conversation, thereby wasting valuable time. Some people tell a story that seems to go on forever, even though it has very little substance. Limit the scope of the question so they'll provide a more concise answer.

Examples of **ineffective** open-ended questions are:

- "I would like to go to Hawaii on vacation, what do you think?" People may assume your mind is made up and just go along, without saying what they prefer.

- "Why are you always picking on me?" People may resent the accusation that they never treat you well.

- "I probably can't do anything about the problems working here, but how are things going anyway?" People may feel you don't care or you're powerless to effect change, so why should they say anything.

In contrast, examples of **effective** open-ended questions are:

- "I would like to go on vacation somewhere that would make us both happy. Can you describe to me what your ideal tropical vacation would look like?" People may feel good about working with you for a win-win.

- "I feel like I'm upsetting you; what am I doing that bothers you?" People may be more open to dealing with conflict when they know you're willing to take some of the responsibility.

- "I want to check in and see how you feel about working here, so how are things going?" People may feel you care about them and will help fix problems.

CLOSED-ENDED. A closed-ended question typically has a "yes" or "no" answer. An explanation with details is not needed, just a response. The advantage of a closed-ended question is speed. You get an answer quickly without having a long conversation. The disadvantage is that the person might feel you're interrogating them, versus having a conversation. Many people won't give a short answer to a closed-ended question. They may not understand the question, why you're asking, or dodge it by changing the subject. Some people are just long-winded and love to hear themselves talk.

Examples of **ineffective** closed-ended questions are:

- "I'm hungry; is dinner ready yet?" People may feel rushed and unappreciated.

- "Are you finished yet?" People may feel resentment because you're hounding them to get their work done faster.

- "Are you ready to go yet?" People may feel rushed and put off with your impatience.

In contrast, examples of **effective** closed-ended questions are:

- "Will we be eating soon or should I have a snack?" People will understand you aren't rushing them, and will appreciate you for taking care of yourself.

- "Is there anything I can do to help finish your work?" People will understand you aren't hounding them; you just want to know if they need assistance.

- "I want to be ready when you are; how long do I have to get ready?" People will realize you aren't impatient; you just want to be ready when they are.

KEY POINTS. The key points of asking effective questions are:

- GET TO THE POINT. Ask a concise question and don't ramble. If you take too long to get to the point then people will be dismissive and tune you out.

- EXPLAIN WHY. Explain why you're asking the question. People will respond with better information when they understand what you want to know. You might even learn something new.

- ASK THE RIGHT QUESTION. You may have heard the expression, "the question behind the question", meaning a question that is really asking something else. Sometimes we may not be clear about what a person is asking. A wife may ask her husband if she looks nice. He may think she's being overly self-critical, but what she really wants to know is if he is attracted to her. A boss may ask what the employees are doing. The employees may think they're in trouble, but what the boss really wants to know is if they need any assistance. A prospective employer may ask about the relationship with your previous boss. What the employer really wants to know is how you respond to authority and if you are a good fit on his team. The advantage of skirting around an issue is that it's a great way to get information. The disadvantage is that the other person has to guess what you really want to know, and may guess wrong. If you're unclear about a question, then reply, "What is it that you really want to know so I can give the best answer?"

- WAIT FOR THE ANSWER. An effective question doesn't provide the answer while asking it. Don't ask, "The problem is poor quality, do you agree?" Ask instead, "What do you think the problem is?" This helps to keep an open mind about the opinions of other people. After asking the question, stop talking and listen. Wait until they are done and don't talk over them. If you ask a question and people think you're not listening to their answer, then they'll feel you don't care, and won't give all the information they have.

- LISTEN AND LEARN. Ask an effective question, listen to the answer, and suspend judgment. Be intent on what people are really saying, and be aware of what the thoughts and feelings are behind their words. Temporarily let go of opinions so they don't block you from learning more information. In addition, listen to what is **not** said. Sometimes there is more information in what people are not saying than what you are hearing. Ask probing questions to uncover hidden meaning and to clarify any misunderstanding.

Deliver On the Promise

When the boss gives a task, our first reaction is to say "yes" because we want to do our jobs well. It's just as easy to say "yes" and set expectations. For example, "Yes and when do you need it?" Notice there is no "buts" in the sentence. Always set expectations before accepting the task. The boss will perceive you as a team player, and a positive attitude will earn the respect of others.

If you cannot meet the deadline because of workload, then establish its priority. Ask, "What can we reschedule or take off my plate?" If they reply, "When can you get it done?" never assume it's a high priority. Always ask for more time than needed. For example, if it sounds like they need it tomorrow then ask for a deadline next week. This gives time to catch up on other high priority tasks in your queue. You'll be amazed how often a later time is acceptable. If they are fair, then they'll work with you to prioritize the task. If not, then ask for more resources (time, people, or money) to get it done.

If all else fails, then set the expectation that you cannot meet the deadline without shifting priorities or having more resources. Most people will be respectful and work with you to find a place in the queue. You are accountable for your own destiny. Don't allow others to choose it for you. Always deliver on the promise!

Those that are most slow in making a promise are the most faithful in the performance of it.

—Jean Jacques Rousseau

No Surprises

No surprises means if you cannot deliver on the promise then change the expectation, **before** the deadline. Too often, we don't want others to know about our inabilities or mistakes. Sometimes things change that are out of our control. Other times we may need more resources to meet the deadline.

Surprises are foolish things. The pleasure is not enhanced, and the inconvenience is often considerable.

—Jane Austen

How to Add Value

When given a task, you add value by clarifying the task and providing more than expected. For example, the boss may ask you to produce a report. The first effective question to ask is, "I want to do a good job, so can you tell me who it's for, when do they need it, and how will they use it? Added Value Support is not only what you do, it's the value you bring. Invest in Yourself by providing Added Value Support to others!

You don't get paid for the hour. You get paid for the value you bring to the hour.

—Jim Rohn

KEY POINTS. Added Value Support includes the following:

- Ask **who** it's for.
  - Knowing who the target audience is will determine how you perform the task and how to present the results.
- Ask **why** they need it.
  - Understand the underlying motivation and need for the task so you're aware of its importance and timing.
- Ask **how** they will use it.
  - The answer will tell you what to focus on, and what to filter out.
- Ask **when** they need it.
  - If you can't meet the deadline, then negotiate a different one before starting the task.
- Think about what they **really** need to know, but didn't ask.
  - Ask clarifying questions before you begin. Start on the right track.
- Think about what **added value** to bring.
  - Find ways to do more than is expected.
- Provide **accurate**, **concise**, and **timely** results.
  - Be on time and accurate; don't ramble on when presenting the results.

ELEVATOR PITCH	
1	**Differentiate Yourself**
2	Who you are, your background, why someone should hire you
3	Have a formal version for business and a casual one for friends
4	Keep it concise, under one minute, the time for an elevator ride
5	**Key Points of the Pitch**
6	Begin with a catch phrase
7	Explain what you do
8	Relate your education and experience
9	Share your interests
10	Close by tying it all back to your catch phrase
11	**Perfect Practice Makes Perfect**
12	Write it down, memorize it, and practice with *Your People*

ELEVATOR PITCH

A valuable skill that will differentiate you from others is presenting an effective elevator pitch. An elevator pitch is a concise summary of who you are, and why someone should hire you. It should be no longer than the time it would take for an elevator ride, under one minute. Have a formal version ready for job interviews and business networking functions. An informal version is better for casual encounters with others who can help achieve your goals.

Always remember that you are absolutely unique. Just like everyone else.

— *Margaret Mead*

MY PITCH. My elevator pitch begins with an introduction and a catch phrase, "Professional Problem Solver." This is quite effective to get the attention of the audience. In the middle, the pitch continues with two options on how to present it. The first is for a job interview, the second for introductions. I end the pitch by tying it all back to my catch phrase. It takes me about 40 seconds to present this pitch. Create your own version and have it "in your hip pocket" when needed.

My elevator pitch goes like this:

"Hello, my name is Jim Dreher and I'm a Professional Problem Solver!"

"I am a Business Consultant with Hewlett-Packard's Technology Services Division. I help customers solve their I.T. problems by designing lifecycle solutions. I hold undergraduate degrees in Technology and Business Management, a graduate degree in Project Management, and I'm a certified Project Management Professional."

Option 1: "I'm seeking an opportunity that is a match for my..."

Option 2: "I have a..."

"...unique depth and breadth of experience in computer programming and repair, service delivery management, and project management. Outside of work, I enjoy my family, music, magic, travel, and golf; and I'm the leader of volunteer groups at church where my problem solving skills are frequently used!"

PRACTICE YOUR PITCH. Write down your elevator pitch, memorize it, and practice with **Your People**. As Lou Tice would say, "Practice doesn't make perfect; perfect practice makes perfect!" Perfect practice will increase confidence when talking about yourself. People will want to get to know more about you—or hire you!

STORIES ON SELF-INVESTMENT

The following stories are on this chapter, *Invest in Yourself*:
- Panic to Power
- Saving Lives
- An Extra Push

Panic to Power

Caroline is a self-employed marketing consultant, and balances her professional life with her loving husband and their two beautiful daughters. Her education and training turned out to be a self-investment that paid dividends in several ways. Here is her story.

"I've always been a big believer in formal education as key to my career aspirations. Going to university and completing a master's degree allowed me to work in the field of social sciences in a meaningful way, in the area of social research. Furthermore, I loved learning. Engaging in discussion with peers and professors opened my thinking to new possibilities and connections that I hadn't previously considered.

A couple of years after I graduated, I was hired for an evaluation position at a prominent philanthropic foundation. Evaluation was new to me at the time, although I had spent the past year purposefully developing my knowledge in this area. I felt so fortunate to land such an exciting, meaningful job in an innovative organization, though I often felt that everyone else on the job was 'smarter', more 'talented' and certainly more qualified than myself. Those first six months on the job, I suffered deeply from imposter syndrome.

Everyone was looking to me as an expert in evaluation, to guide and inform their processes and decisions. After all, isn't that why they hired me? Little did they know, I had only a year of experience under my belt. Every time I went to a meeting or was solicited for advice, I panicked that my colleagues would find me out and realize that I really didn't know what I was talking about. I often began and ended my conversations or meetings with "but I haven't been here very long" as a way of putting off people's expectations of me.

One day, I was in a meeting with a senior colleague, discussing strategies for a project we were working on together. I felt out of my depth, and quickly turned to my favorite line "I'm new, so am not sure I can answer that." She looked me in the eye, and said, "You've been here six months. You're no longer new. You need to decide to step up to the plate and start owning your role."

I was mortified. The embarrassment I felt by being called out by a senior colleague almost prompted me to leave that meeting room and never come back! I left work that day with her scolding heavy on my mind. Once I got past my own ego, I realized she was right. It was time for me to start stepping up, and move from a place of panic to a place of power.

Sometimes, we can get caught up in our own self talk. I had spent so much time thinking about what everyone else was capable of, and the experience everyone else had, that I neglected to invest time thinking about and believing in what I was capable of. By also spending time pretending to know everything, I had closed myself to seizing opportunities for learning and growth.

After some reflection, I went back and thanked my colleague for her honesty. I also opened myself up and asked her thoughts on where I could improve and grow. I approached the situation as I would have back in graduate school, with excitement about the new possibilities that learning and pushing myself could bring.

Now, when I come into new situations I start from the place of "what can I learn" as opposed to "what do I have to prove." This mindset has opened me up to a world of possibilities. Collaboration with colleagues is easier and more meaningful because I am eager to experience what they have to teach me. I am less fearful about protecting my "turf" because diverse thinking really does contribute to a better product in the end.

While University did provide me with some real tangible skills, the greatest skill it gave me was the appreciation of learning—and how continuous learning propels you much further professionally and personally than maintaining the status quo. I was able to turn panic into power!"

> *Having a mindset for growth is the key to turn panic into power.*
>
> —*Caroline Claussen*

Saving Lives

Mark is a paramedic firefighter who lives with his wife and two teenage children. He enjoys family activities, sports, camping, and is active at his church. Mark took the time to invest in himself to get where he is today. The many people he has helped over his career are thankful he did! Here is his story.

"At age seventeen, I worked a summer job as lifeguard at a water amusement park. Achieving my lifeguard certification was hard work. I took many classes including CPR, water safety, and live saving. The training was a challenge but it really paid off. I became a skilled lifeguard and I really enjoyed helping people stay safe in the water.

I became friends with another lifeguard who was also an Emergency Medical Technician (EMT). After seeing him in action, I decided that's what I wanted to become. It was a natural progression from my lifeguard training to an EMT. The next year, I enrolled in college for my certification and for new challenges.

After graduating, I worked as an EMT with paramedics from a large fire department. I soon realized that as much as I enjoyed being an EMT, I wanted to become a firefighter even more! It was beneficial to be a paramedic first, so I enrolled in training. I completed my paramedic certification and joined an ambulance company. I worked at local firehouses running calls during the same 24-hour shifts as the firefighters.

My passion to become a firefighter grew and eventually my chief sponsored me to attend the fire academy. I was older than most of the other students and married with one child. We had a mortgage so we both worked fulltime. I attended the fire academy three days per week including weekends. I enjoyed the hands-on training and physical challenge, and graduated at the top of my class. I found my purpose, but firefighter jobs were scarce in my area.

Several people were coaching me how to land a firefighter job. My neighbor was a firefighter who gave me help, support, and encouragement to remain persistent and achieve my goal. I made a promise for the future that if someone ever came to me, then I would help them the same way my neighbor helped me. As it turns out, having both paramedic and firefighter training was the key to landing my first job.

A day in the life of a paramedic firefighter starts in the morning when I arrive at the station. I instinctively realize I'm no longer at home so I shift into a routine at work. I meet with peers going off-duty to understand what happened the night before, so I know what equipment to check and what first aid inventory to re-stock. Then the equipment is loaded on the rig, and we do training, maintenance, inspections, physical fitness, and other chores throughout the day. We eat meals together at the station, then after dinner it's down time for school, special projects, and catch-up. Finally, it's bedtime and lights-out at ten pm.

Oh, by the way, every call that comes in during the 24-hour shift interrupts this routine. Sometimes it's tough, but I do manage to get an average of four hours of intermittent sleep per shift. Generally, I have four shifts in a rack of seven days. The shifts can be grueling, but the comradery of my peers and knowing that we save lives every day makes it all worthwhile!

Over the past twenty years, I've had the privilege to help many Explorer scouts and other paramedic students. I've helped them with paramedic theory, mock interviews, what's on the exam, and tips for their physical fitness. I've kept my promise that if people ever came to me then I would help them the same way others helped me

Recently, I was helping a paramedic student who knew everything taught in school, but would freeze up when treating a patient. Classroom teaching is great, but when treating a real life patient in crisis, a paramedic must be able to think and act or a life could be lost. Getting excited and doing something irrational makes the problem worse. It takes the experience of multiple patients to learn rational thinking in such situations. My advice was simple but profound. Start by taking a deep breath and relax. Focus and eliminate distractions. Next, think of doing it on paper, and then do it on the patient. He took my advice and turned his performance around to become number one in his class. After working with him for a while, I can honestly say that I would allow him to work on my family, even in a crisis.

Speaking of a crisis, I'll always remember the first time I delivered a baby. I was just out of High School, and only two months out of EMT school. My ambulance partner and I received a call for a wellness check, not an emergency. We arrived to find a woman in her late twenties who was pregnant and starting to have contractions. We weren't worried because the hospital was only five miles away. By the time she was on the gurney and in the back of the ambulance, I heard her groan and say, "It's coming!" I looked down and was shocked to see the baby's head crowning. I was a young EMT, not a paramedic. My partner was more experienced, but never delivered a baby. I instinctively did what I trained to do. I took a deep breath, relaxed, and followed the textbook approach as I went over the checklist in my head. I was relieved to deliver the first of over fifty babies during my career!

Another time, I got a call to the scene of a car crash. A woman was in cardiac arrest, and the first responders started CPR. I took over as the senior medic but she was not responding. I shocked her twice to get her heartbeat back. Her treatment and care continued at the hospital and was discharged a week later. I received an award from the city and State Legislature for not giving up, and reviving someone who was clinically dead over ten minutes. I appreciate the award, but I do this on a routine basis so it was a bit awkward to receive recognition for just doing my job.

One of my most memorable calls was a sixteen-year-old girl who delivered her baby daughter in a bathroom stall. The baby was premature at only twenty weeks and was the length of my middle finger to my wrist. I performed CPR, inserted a breathing tube, and then transported both to the hospital. Fourteen years later, I was in a hospital and the same woman, who I did not recognize, said she wanted to thank me. She introduced me to her daughter who was there with her. The premature baby whose life I saved had grown into a beautiful young woman. Moments like that make me feel incredible and give me the drive to continue. It warms my heart to know that people still care about what you do.

My story is about how I invested in myself to accomplish my goals and to be the best team member I can be. Our team at the fire service is similar to teams in other jobs. We use our positive attitudes, mentoring, and the Golden Rule to get along with each and get the job done. However, other jobs are about production and saving costs. In our case, it's about saving lives!"

It warms my heart to know that people still care about what you do.

—*Mark MacDonald*

An Extra Push

I was 16 when I was on the High School swim team. Swimming was enjoyable because it was the only sport I was any good at. Not only was I a strong swimmer, but also looked great in a swimsuit! My greatest achievement was at the State Championships. Although I didn't take first place, I was very proud of my results. I competed against thousands of swimmers and finished in the top ten. It still feels great today, and I learned some important life lessons leading up to it.

I was a sophomore on the team and second best in the breaststroke. My goal was to beat the best who was, of course, a senior. He was more mature, experienced, and looked better in a swimsuit. I'll never forget the day we were racing and I was winning! I was in the zone. The team was excited and screaming for their favorite to finish first! The coach was walking along the side of the pool and yelling, "Go—go—go!" I was smooth and fast, and he was struggling to keep up with me. I had him now. The "thrill of victory" was mine!

My final stroke was exactly what I practiced hundreds of times; keep my momentum and glide into the finish. At the same time, I looked over and saw him lunge as he pushed his fingertips into the wall. I came up for air, looked at the results board, and then just floated there in the "agony of defeat."

He was very kind and actually thanked me for the motivation to make him dig deep. He explained how he was losing his interest in the sport, but now has some competition and his passion is back. I gained a friend that day, and earned the respect of the entire team and coaching staff.

The lessons are; learn from experience, perfect practice makes perfect, and a defeat can be turned into a victory. From time to time, I think back on that day and use the lessons learned for success in my personal and professional life. An extra "push" at the end can make all the difference!

REFLECT ON SELF-INVESTMENT

Reflect on the following and discuss with *Your People:*

1. How do I invest in myself?
2. Am I comfortable asking others for help?
3. Why does appearance matter?
4. What have others said about my appearance?
5. How have I invested in myself with education and training?
6. What goals have I set to develop my skills?
7. What is Added Value Support?
8. How can I anticipate the needs of other people?
9. What is the difference between an effective question and an ineffective one?
10. What is the difference between a closed-ended and open-ended question?
11. What does "Deliver on the Promise" mean?
12. When was the last time I surprised my boss by not keeping him or her informed?
13. In what ways can I add value?
14. Do I have an elevator pitch?
15. Can I recite my elevator pitch from memory?

LIVE A BALANCED LIFE	
	LIVE A BALANCED LIFE
1	**Balance With Self**
2	Emotional, mental, physical, religious, and social health
3	Treat yourself well and feel good, but not at the expense of others
4	*Your People* will advise about your attitude and behavior
5	**Balance With Others**
6	I treat others the way (I want or they want) to be treated
7	Get to know others and you'll learn how to treat them
8	Resign your commission as "Captain of the World"
9	**Balance With Relationships**
10	Build relationships; don't just network, also build friendships
11	Value diversity and inclusion; you'll see the world differently
12	Do the right thing; what is right for others and yourself

4. LIVE A BALANCED LIFE

The previous chapters were on how to achieve success by selecting your attitude, managing goals, and investing in yourself. This chapter is on balancing success with the other aspects of life. In his popular book, *Maximum Achievement*, acclaimed success guru Brian Tracy stresses that balance is one of the critical areas of life. He compares life with the wheels on a car; both must be in balance to run smoothly. You live a balanced life by achieving success while feeling good about yourself, and other people.

> *Just as your car runs more smoothly and requires less energy to go faster and farther when the wheels are in perfect alignment, you perform better when your thoughts, feelings, emotions, goals, and values are in balance.*
>
> —*Brian Tracy*

IT'S A JOURNEY. A balanced life manages resources (time, money, people, and possessions), without one or more dominating at the expense of the others. In theory, you live a balanced life by dividing time equally between work, home, and play—each with equal resources. In reality, a balanced life is a journey, not a destination.

> *When you dance, your purpose is not to get to a certain place on the floor. It's to enjoy each step along the way.*
>
> —*Wayne Dyer*

IT'S A CHALLENGE. It's a challenge to live in balance all the time. Some goals require a temporary focus in certain areas of life at the expense of others. It's okay not to have everything and do everything at the same time. Acknowledge imperfection, strive for improvement, and enjoy the journey!

> *I've learned that you can't have everything and do everything at the same time.*
>
> —*Oprah Winfrey*

GOALS FOR BALANCE. When setting a goal that causes an imbalance, also include a plan of how to get it back into balance. For example, family may support you in devoting more time at work on an important project. Then after it's complete, the family will go on a planned vacation. You can always work harder and make more money, but you cannot make more time. Time is precious, limited, and irreplaceable; and so is your family!

> *Remember, you can earn more money, but when time is spent is gone forever.*
>
> —*Zig Ziglar*

STRIVE FOR BALANCE. Living a balanced life is an easy concept to understand, but can be difficult to achieve. Even when you do achieve it, it may not last. Don't stop striving for balance. **Your People** can help you acknowledge and correct imbalances in life that may occur from time to time.

> *Life is like riding a bicycle. To keep your balance you must keep moving.*
>
> —*Albert Einstein*

BALANCE WITH SELF

Having balance means to feel good about yourself, but not at the expense of others. Treat yourself well. Only then will you know what it feels like when treating others the same.

> *I treat myself the way I want others to treat me.*
>
> —*Variation of the Golden Rule*

In All Areas

For a more balanced life, let go of problems and focus on opportunities. Doing so will increase confidence in others and yourself. Few people can achieve balance all the time. However, many people achieve success when they give up control, acknowledge imperfection, and strive for balance.

> *As your faith is strengthened, you will find that there is no longer the need to have a sense of control, that things will flow as they will, and that you will flow with them, to your great delight and benefit.*
>
> —*Emmanuel Teney*

KEY POINTS. The key points on balance in all areas of life are:

- EMOTIONAL. Manage anger, resolve conflict, and control your behavior.
- MENTAL. Your psychological well-being.
- PHYSICAL. Diet and exercise under the supervision of your physician.
- FAITH. Being at peace with your spirituality and religion.
- SOCIAL. Positive relationships and the support of **Your People**.

Self-Image

Self-image is the opinion we have of ourselves. We form our self-image largely based on expectations. Positive expectations can be a self-fulfilling prophecy. If we expect to succeed, then we are more likely to succeed than those who expect to fail.

> *The person we believe ourselves to be will always act in a manner consistent with our self-image.*
>
> —*Brian Tracy*

KEY POINTS. The key points on the opinion we have of ourselves are:

- SELF-IMAGE
  - The mental picture of yourself that's resistant to change.
  - "What do I believe people think about me?"
- SELF-WORTH
  - The feeling that you are a good person who deserves respect.
  - "I deserve to be treated with respect."
- SELF-ESTEEM
  - The belief about your worth; based sometimes on emotion versus fact.
  - "I feel pride in being a competent and worthy person."
- SELF-COMPASSION
  - Extending compassion to yourself after a setback.
  - "I'm kind to myself when I make a mistake."

Self-Compassion

A recent study, published by researchers Breines and Chen, reports that self-compassion may increase the motivation to succeed. The study shows that people who are accountable for their failure may be more motivated to improve themselves. Select an Attitude of Accountability, and have compassion for yourself after a setback!

> *We should remember that just as a positive outlook on life can promote good health, so can everyday acts of kindness.*
> —*Hillary Clinton*

KEY POINTS. The key points on self-compassion are:

- Self-compassion may increase motivation to succeed.
- Accepting failure may create motivation for improvement.
- Select an Attitude of Accountability.
- Have compassion for yourself after a setback.

BALANCE WITH OTHERS

Having balance with others means getting along with people. Few people achieve success on their own. In contrast, most successful people build strong relationships.

> *Personal relationships are the fertile soil from which all advancement, all success, all achievement in real life grows.*
>
> —*Ben Stein*

BALANCE FOR SUCCESS. I believe that winning is getting the entire team across the finish line. I believe the same thing about success. True success is helping everyone achieve his or her goals.

> *I believe that being successful means having a balance of success stories across the many areas of your life. You can't truly be considered successful in your business life if your home life is in shambles.*
>
> —*Zig Ziglar*

Do the Right Thing

Many organizations include these four words in their policy and procedures manual: do the right thing. Most business experts agree that success stems from doing what is right. One well-known business expert is Meg Whitman, former CEO of eBay and current CEO of Hewlett-Packard. In her insightful book, *The Power of Many*, she tells a story about walking in on a noisy meeting of her senior staff. They were disagreeing over what to do about an important financial issue. Meg simply asked, "What is the **right** thing to do here?" Then she left the room. The debate ended immediately and her staff agreed on a plan to address the issue. Ask yourself the same question when not sure what to do about a problem. In all situations, decide what is right for others and yourself, commit to that right thing, then do it!

> *Do the right thing. It will gratify some people and astonish the rest.*
>
> —*Mark Twain*

YOU KNOW WHAT TO DO. Over time, you'll learn what the right thing to do is in each situation. Do the right thing and accept the consequences. If you're ever in doubt then involve *Your People*.

> *The truth of the matter is that you always know the right thing to do. The hard part is doing it.*
> —*Robert H. Schuller*

SO DO IT. Sometimes doing the right thing means to have courage and speak the truth rather than remain silent. You will learn whether to say something or not. Select Your Attitude, make a choice, and be accountable for the outcome. Be a Doer and do the right thing!

> *You are not only responsible for what you say, but also for what you do not say.*
> —*Martin Luther*

The Golden Rule

The ethic of reciprocity is a concept that is in common with nearly all philosophy, psychology, sociology, and religions of the world. Most people know this as The Golden Rule. I think its great advice and I strive to use it daily.

> *I treat others the way I want them to treat me.*
> —*Golden Rule*

The Platinum Rule

The Golden Rule may not apply to everyone. Some people don't want to be treated the way you do. In his popular book, *The Platinum Rule*, Dr. Tony Alessandra says that sometimes you have to treat others the way **they** would want, not the way **you** would want. Knowing how to treat others requires empathy by putting yourself in their shoes, or by simply asking them.

> *I treat others the way they want to be treated.*
> —*The Platinum Rule*

KNOW OTHERS. Get to know more about people and learn how to treat them. It's easy to assume the worst about others, especially if you deal with them online or on the phone versus in person. Nevertheless, why would we assume anything when we can get to know them instead? When you begin a new relationship, especially if it's not in person, be sure to take the time up front to develop a good rapport with each other. Find something in common and develop goodwill that you may need later to prevail over conflict.

> *The way you see people is the way you treat them, and the way you treat them is what they become.*
>
> —*Johann Wolfgang von Goethe*

HELP OTHERS. Manage your resources to help others with charity and volunteering. I've seen many strong relationships develop while volunteering. Both people are there to serve others and are more open to becoming interested in each other. It's especially heart-warming to see children let down their guard and improve their bond with their parents and each other. Some of the greatest joy and satisfaction I've received is when I've volunteered to help others. I encourage everyone to help other people. You don't have to do anything that takes a lot of time or money. Start by helping just one person.

> *We can't help everyone, but everyone can help someone.*
>
> —*Ronald Reagan*

EMPATHY FOR OTHERS. Whether you adopt the Golden Rule, Platinum Rule, or both, having empathy for others is always the right thing to do.

> *We live in a culture that discourages empathy. A culture that too often tells us our principle goal in life is to be rich, thin, young, famous, safe, and entertained.*
>
> —*Barack Obama*

RESOLVE CONFLICT	
1	**Select Your Attitude**
2	Assume the best, realize good intentions, be accountable
3	**Manage Your Goals**
4	Use the Six P's to research, define, and resolve the problem
5	**Invest in Yourself**
6	Learn communication, negotiation, and resolution techniques
7	**Live a Balanced Life**
8	Extend compassion to others and yourself
9	Do the right thing; build relationships
10	Use P.L.U.T.O. Communication
11	**Embrace Change**
12	Acknowledge the change that led to the conflict

Resolve Conflict

Conflict, it seems, is inevitable. It stems from differences in values, beliefs, and actions. It's normal to have conflict with other people in our personal and professional relationships. In their comprehensive book, *Resolving Conflicts at Work: Ten Strategies for Everyone on the Job*, experts Kenneth Cloke and Joan Goldsmith assert that there are positive and negative aspects of conflict. Conflict may have a negative outcome when not dealt with in the right way. On the other hand, conflict may have a positive outcome if dealt with in a constructive manner.

> *Every conflict we face in life is rich with positive and negative potential. It can be a source of inspiration, enlightenment, learning, transformation, and growth–or rage, fear, shame, entrapment, and resistance. The choice is not up to our opponents, but to us, and our willingness to face and work through them.*
>
> —Kenneth Cloke and Joan Goldsmith

142

COMMUNICATION. Living a balanced life means learning to deal with other people and resolve conflict. The key is learning how to communicate effectively. **Your People** will give constructive feedback on how well you communicate with others.

> *People fail to get along because they fear each other; they fear each other because they don't know each other; they don't know each other because they have not communicated with each other.*

> —*Martin Luther King Jr.*

FEEDBACK. If one person gives feedback about your attitude or behavior then it's an opinion. If you get the same feedback from several others, then it's a common perception of the truth. When in doubt, **Your People** will advise if you have any attitude or behavior issues.

> *Individuals need to be willing to face truth about their attitudes, behaviors, even what we want out of life.*

> —*Joyce Meyer*

When to Do Something

Learning how to resolve conflict without emotional injury is vital for happiness and success. Do this by selecting your attitude and assume the best in people. Realize everyone's good intentions and desire for a positive outcome. **Your People** are there to help resolve conflict.

> *Whenever you're in conflict with someone, there is one factor that can make the difference between damaging your relationship and deepening it. That factor is attitude.*

> —*William James*

RESOLVE CONFLICT.   There are several possible outcomes of conflict resolution, including the following:

- COLLABORATING
  - "Win/Win."
  - Nothing is lost and all sides come out with a win.
  - Use when you trust each other to share responsibility.
- COMPROMISING
  - "Win Some/Lose Some."
  - Each side loses a little yet all come out with an acceptable resolution.
  - Use when the "common good" is more important.
- ACCOMMODATING
  - "Lose/Win."
  - One side loses; the other side wins.
  - Use when it's not that important or when you were wrong.
- COMPETING
  - "Win/Lose."
  - One side wins; the other loses.
  - Use when the outcome is more important than the relationship.
- AVOIDING
  - "No Winners/No Losers."
  - Neither side wins or loses.
  - Use when it's not the right time or place, or if the conflict will resolve itself.

POSITIVE OUTCOMES.   The two key positive outcomes of conflict resolution are collaboration and compromise. Collaboration is the most positive because both sides build trust and come out with a "win". Compromise is positive as long as one side is not just "giving in" and regretting it later. Each side gives a little, yet all come out with an acceptable resolution.

Alone we can do so little; together we can do so much.
—Helen Keller

KEY POINTS. The key points of when to do something to resolve conflict are:

- SELECT YOUR ATTITUDE
  - Assume the best in people and realize everyone's good intentions for a positive resolution.
  - Be accountable for your actions, behaviors, and choices.
- MANAGE YOUR GOALS
  - Prepare: Gather information about the problem and the other people.
  - Plan: Discuss what the problem is about, and agree on a written definition.
  - Perform: Schedule meetings to work out differences.
  - Prevail: Be patient and persistent; work through temporary setbacks.
  - Produce: Achieve the goal: collaborate, compromise, accommodate, compete, or avoid.
  - Perfect: Use lessons learned for continuous improvement.
- INVEST IN YOURSELF
  - Learn communication, negotiation, and conflict resolution techniques.
  - Leverage Added Value Support methods: anticipate needs, ask effective questions, deliver on the promise, no surprises, and do more than expected.
  - Practice with *Your People*.
- LIVE A BALANCE LIVE
  - Extend compassion to others and yourself. Remain calm, be patient, have empathy and respect.
  - Do the Right Thing. Decide what is right for others and yourself, commit to that right thing, then do it!
  - Build Relationships. Use your interpersonal skills to build relationships.
  - Use P.L.U.T.O. Communication): Prepare, Listen, Understand, Timing, and Observe (discussed later in this chapter).

- EMBRACE CHANGE
  - Anticipate changes that may lead to conflict.
  - Acknowledge change when it occurs during the resolution process.
  - Accept change by adapting with it.

When to Do Nothing

Sometimes the right thing to do is nothing at all! Conflict with others, and with yourself, can be stressful. You're in conflict when you take on too much, and cannot get it all done on time. Balance with others and your health will improve from less conflict and stress. You will learn when the right thing to do is nothing.

> *To do nothing at all is the most difficult thing in the world, the most difficult and the most intellectual.*
>
> —*Oscar Wilde*

DON'T PARTICIPATE. Doing nothing doesn't mean being idle or lazy. It's good for your health to avoid conflict and take a break by slowing down, both physically and mentally. Sometimes conflict is best resolved by not participating in it.

> *Conflict cannot survive without your participation.*
>
> —*Wayne Dyer*

SMALL STUFF. Perhaps Dr. Richard Carlson said it best about when to do nothing in his best-selling book, *Don't Sweat the Small Stuff…and it's all Small Stuff*. He says don't get worked up about the small things in life, and don't blow up problems out of proportion. I agree; don't lose your precious, limited, and irreplaceable time sweating the small stuff.

> *Don't sweat over the small stuff … it's all small stuff.*
>
> —*Dr. Richard Carlson*

KEY POINTS. The key points of when to do nothing are:

- TECH STRESS. The good thing about technology is that we can choose when to respond. Rarely do we have to respond instantly. The bad thing is that people are conditioned to respond when they receive a reward. In a recent Harvard study, Tamir and Mitchell find that disclosing information about ourselves is inherently rewarding. For example, the pleasure you get from reading or sending a personal text message. Resist the urge to respond immediately to text or email messages, and think of relaxation as your reward.

- SOCIAL MEDIA ADDICTION. Recent studies conclude that many people are literally becoming addicted to email, texting, and other social media. Dr. Susan Moeller of the University of Maryland supervised *The World Unplugged* research study. The study shows that students from around the world couldn't go without using social media for just 24 hours. Select an Attitude of Choice and an Attitude of Accountability to avoid social media addiction.

- FOMO. The fear of missing out is "FOMO". Slow down and say "no" sometimes. Take time to do what you want, not what other people want you to do.

- CREATIVITY. Take "offline" time by yourself just to think creatively. Some examples of "offline" time include: brainstorm, daydream, journal, meditate, music, sleep, and a walk in the park.

- LETITGO. The words "let it go" slurred together intentionally is "Letitgo". When the consequence is low, then sometimes the best thing to do is nothing. If someone makes an accusation or nasty comment, you don't have to respond. If people bring problems, ask them what they would do. They'll figure it out for themselves, and all will benefit.

Build Relationships

Success comes from building relationships. The best relationships are when we show interest by sharing and listening to each other. It amazes me how many people I meet with "I-itis". They love to talk about only one thing all the time—themselves. Carnegie emphasizes in his highly regarded book, *How to Win Friends and Influence People*, the secret to getting people to do what you want is to give them what they want. He advises that if you want other people to like you, then show an authentic interest in them.

> *You can make more friends in two months by becoming interested in other people than you can in two years by trying to get other people interested in you.*
>
> —*Dale Carnegie*

NETWORKING. Don't just network; build friendships and relationships. Networking may be the most effective way to get a new job. However, if you're always asking friends for something without giving something in return, it can hurt the friendship. Instead, be a friend first and build a relationship. Let friends know what you need and return their friendship by helping them when they need it.

> *The richest people in the world look for and build networks, everyone else looks for work.*
>
> —*Robert Kiyosaki*

HELP OTHERS. Use your experience to help others; it's a great way to start a friendship.

> *What do we live for, if it is not to make life less difficult for each other?*
>
> —*George Eliot*

COMMUNICATION. Building relationships requires good interpersonal skills. The ability to communicate and get along with other people is paramount for success. Whether at home, work, or play, you'll always be dealing with others. Develop your interpersonal skills and use them to build meaningful relationships with other people.

> *Eighty percent of life's satisfaction comes from meaningful relationships.*
>
> —*Brian Tracy*

CHOOSE YOUR RESPONSE. In addition to getting along with others, interpersonal skills can help us choose our response when we aren't treated the way we want to be treated. We use our skills to respond, not react. In doing so, we build people up and make them feel better about themselves, and better about us.

> *People will forget what you said, they will forget what you did, but they will never forget how you made them feel.*
> —*Maya Angelou*

KEY POINTS. The key interpersonal skills to learn and develop are:
- Anger Management
- Communication and Listening
- Conflict Resolution
- Critical Thinking
- Influence / Negotiation / Persuasion
- Problem Solving
- Teamwork

Captain of the World

We can use interpersonal skills to avoid finding fault in other people. It's easy to find fault in others. Other people could be smarter, faster, more efficient, and more responsible, so **why aren't they trying harder?**

> *It is much easier to find fault with others, than to be faultless ourselves.*
> —*Samuel Richardson*

RESIGN YOUR COMMISSION. Some people believe they are empowered to enforce the "rules" and tell others how they should behave. A person who often finds fault in others is what Lou Tice calls a "Captain of the World." **Your People** will advise if you're a Captain of the World. If they do, then raise your right hand and ask them to accept your resignation immediately!

> *Repeat after me; I hereby resign from being the Captain of the World. Now go out and act like it!*
> —*Lou Tice*

P.L.U.T.O. COMMUNICATION	
1	**P**repare; research the facts and have your positions ready
2	**L**isten; internalize what their words mean, don't talk over them
3	**U**nderstand; clarify by repeating back what you heard
4	**T**iming; is everything, wait for an appropriate time and place
5	**O**bserve; look into their eyes and watch their body language
6	
7	**Listen and Observe**
8	Sometimes it's more important to listen for what is **not** said
9	People tend to skirt around an issue
10	Learn to interpret hidden thoughts and feelings
11	Observe body language and the tone of their voice
12	**Get to Know Others and You Will Learn How to Treat Them**

P.L.U.T.O. Communication

Did you know that Pluto is smaller than Earth's moon and is barely visible to the Hubble Space Telescope? So what does Pluto have to do with communication? Absolutely nothing! It's just a simple acronym whose letters nicely match the key points I want to convey.

Then again, Pluto is the furthest dwarf planet from Earth, representing how far apart we can be when we are trying to communicate. Also, there has recently been controversy about the reclassification of Pluto from the ninth planet to a dwarf planet, representing how communication can be controversial as well.

Actually, P.L.U.T.O. is a very useful memorization technique called a mnemonic. Mnemonics are audio and visual keys used to remember something. They associate the thing to remember with a word, picture, or sound that you can easily recall from memory.

One thing for sure; Pluto gives us a lot to talk about; and for that, we need communication.

> *Courage is what it takes to stand up and speak; courage is also what it takes to sit down and listen.*
>
> *—Winston Churchill*

150

LISTEN AND OBSERVE. It's important to listen to what other people are saying. Sometimes it's even more important to listen for what they are **not** saying. Many people tend to skirt around an issue and won't come out and plainly say what's on their mind. You don't have to be a mind reader, but learn to interpret hidden thoughts and feelings. Do this by observing the other person's body language and the tone of their voice.

> *The most important thing in communication is hearing what isn't said.*
>
> —*Peter F. Drucker*

KEY POINTS. The key points of "P.L.U.T.O. Communication" are:

- **P**REPARE. Research the topic. Have your facts and positions ready prior to the conversation.

- **L**ISTEN. Internalize what their words mean. Wait until they finish talking before speaking.

- **U**NDERSTAND. Clarify what they say by repeating back what you heard.

- **T**IMING. Timing is everything. Wait for an appropriate time and place. Take a time-out if necessary.

- **O**BSERVE. Look into their eyes so they know you're listening. Watch their body language.

Politically Astute

Being politically astute is not only about being politically correct. And it's certainly not about participating in negative office politics. On the contrary, it's about avoiding negative perceptions from others. "Politically Astute" is to have an Attitude of Accountability for your actions, behaviors, and choices—typically at the workplace.

> *Don't flatter yourselves that friendship authorizes you to say disagreeable things to your intimates. On the contrary, the nearer you come into relation with a person, the more necessary do tact and courtesy become.*
>
> —*Oliver Wendell Holmes, Sr.*

KNOW THE RULES. First, learn what the "rules" are. Then you can choose to follow, bend, or break them if necessary. I'm always careful when I choose to bend or break the rules. I remind myself that I'm accountable for the consequences. Sometimes I ask for permission, and other times I ask for forgiveness. If you've not sure which to choose for a given situation, then ask **Your People** for their advice.

> It is often easier to ask for forgiveness than to ask for permission.
>
> — Grace Hopper

KNOW THE PEOPLE. Successful people learn who to align with, and who to avoid.

- POWER. Who has the real power versus those who think they do.

- ALLIANCES. Make friends and build relationships. Typically the Positive Wizards.

- ENEMIES. Who to avoid or not get too close to. Typically the Negative Wizards.

- ADVANCEMENT. What it takes to get ahead. Select Your Attitude for advancement.

> To know the pains of power, we must go to those who have it. To know its pleasures, we must go to those who are seeking it. The pains of power are real, its pleasures imaginary.
>
> — Charles Caleb Colton

KEY POINTS. The key points of being Politically Astute are:

- KNOW THE RULES. Learn who has the power versus those who think they do. Learn the rules, and learn when to follow, bend, or break them.

- KNOW THE PEOPLE. Learn who to align with, and who to avoid.

- MANAGE YOUR MANAGER. Learn what your superiors like and dislike about the company, the staff, and their senior management. Know what they want versus what they really need. Provide Added Value Support: anticipate needs, set expectations, and then deliver on the promise.

- MANAGE YOURSELF. Avoid a career-limiting move with inappropriate language or behavior. There is a right time and place for humor, having fun, and venting. Learn when, where, and with whom it's appropriate.

- MANAGE OTHERS. Regardless of job title, other people may see you as a leader. They see you know what to do, so they follow your example. You're a Positive Wizard intentionally, or a negative one by accident. Lead by example with an Attitude of Possibility.

Value Diversity

We all live and think differently from each other. Our differences include many things: age, class, ethnic origin, gender, physical and mental ability, race, sexual orientation, spiritual practice, veteran's status, and others. At the same time, we all have things in common. We may have similar values and beliefs, or we may enjoy doing the same things. The goal of valuing diversity is to focus on similarities rather than differences.

Share our similarities, celebrate our differences.

—*M. Scott Peck*

THE MIX OF PEOPLE. Select Your Attitude to value diversity and inclusion. Diversity is the mix of different people, while inclusion is creating an environment for the mix to work well together. Valuing diversity and inclusion will help you see the world in different ways and overcome obstacles on the path to success.

If we cannot end now our differences, at least we can make the world safe for diversity ... we all breathe the same air ... cherish our children's future ... and we are all mortal.

—*John F. Kennedy*

STORIES ON BALANCE

The following stories are on this chapter, *Live a Balanced Life*:

- Always There
- Do the Right Thing
- Differences are Rewarding

Always There

Nicole is a medical transcriber who loves her husband, their son, and her extended family. They enjoy family activities together including camping, car shows, and sports. Her hobbies are cooking, music, movies, family, and she is an avid reader. Nicole and her husband made the decision early in their marriage to live a balance life, and they found a way to accomplish their goal using technology. Here is her story.

"I always had a supportive family growing up. I sure needed that support through High School and college! Mom stayed home and took care of the family while Dad had a career and traveled from time to time. Things changed for me about the time my parents were having problems in their marriage. My major was Psychology and my grades were good, but I was losing interest in it. I loved the human connection aspects of Psych, but the research, statics, and reporting was dull and uninteresting. At some point, finishing school was no longer as important as the extra income I was earning. I wanted to be independent and help my family by not being a financial burden for them.

I left school and took a fulltime job where I met my future husband. We got married and a few years later and had our son. Having a baby changed my life! I used to be responsible only for myself, but now my handsome baby son received all my attention. I was happy to take a back seat and be responsible for him and my husband more than myself.

My father was retired so he moved in with us to care for our son while I went back to work. Just one year later, the economy took a turn for the worse and my company had to lay people off. My job was safe, but I wanted to be with my son and watch every moment as he grows up. I asked to be let go so that someone else could keep their job and I could be at home taking care of my family.

Preschool came and Kindergarten was just around the corner. My husband advanced to a supervisor position at work with a schedule that complements my own. Now it was time to think of my own future so I decide to take classes online. I graduated with honors and earned a medical transcription certificate. Now I'm able to work from home, choose my schedule, enjoy my hobbies, and be close with my family.

Our day is pretty much the same as any working couple with children. However, I am able to shift my work schedule so I care for our son during the day while my husband works, then he takes over at night when I work. We make sure there is plenty of overlap and days off together to share our lives together.

Technology has been great for my work/life balance, but at home, we enjoy activities together more than watching television, using social media, or playing video games. Our son enjoys hanging out with Dad more than watching TV.

I have the flexibility to volunteer once per week and for special occasions at school. School is great for my son and he's learning so much. He should be learning because his daily homework is plentiful! I'm so fortunate that Dad can help with homework every night, and we are both there to support him when he's having a bad day. We're grateful to pass on to our son the family support we had at his age.

We are an extremely happy family and look forward to enjoying the balanced life we have chosen for ourselves. I never thought of myself as setting goals, but I guess I did set this one. I'm grateful to have accomplished my goal and to always be there for my family."

> *Family is always there to support you. You can't go wrong because even if you fail, they are always there!*
>
> —*Nicole Aguilar*

Do the Right Thing

My first assignment as a Project Manager was a multi-million dollar project to stage and deploy computers to all 58 counties in California. I soon realized how much my boss believed in me, because the project had been "red" for some. It was over budget, behind schedule, and needed an emergency fix. Poor quality caused re-work both at the staging center and in the field. It didn't take long to find the root cause, the manager of the staging center. I'll call him "John". John needed an immediate improvement, or replacement, to get the project back on track.

I traveled to the staging center to meet with John and his staff on several occasions. His staff was a very dedicated team with excellent ideas how to improve quality. Unfortunately, John felt I was faulting his staff before I even arrived. In retrospect, he was trying to do the right thing for his staff by not cooperating with me. I've met several people like John over the years and I still don't understand how they think doing this will turn out well for them, or their staff. People who know me say I'm "tough, but fair." Well, my fairness tank was empty for John.

I held John solely accountable for the staging center issues. Based on the input from his own team, I showed him how to increase both capacity and quality. He pushed back saying they were doing the best they could—period. After a few uncomfortable meetings, John complained to his boss. His boss worked for my mentor; the same one who invested in me to get the project back on track. John loved his boss dearly and actually kept a picture of his boss on his desk. However, he had no idea his boss couldn't help him now. John was not very politically astute.

John's boss ordered me to fly there the next day to address the complaints against me. I was new in the organization so his boss didn't know me. I didn't know him either, but I knew he was very protective of John. This was my first project manager assignment and one of the largest in the company. If I failed, it would be the end of my career. None of that mattered to me; I knew I had to do the right thing, regardless of the consequences.

I calmly sat and listed for fifteen minutes while John verbally trashed me. His boss took it all in and noticed I wasn't upset at all. He asked me if I had anything to say for myself. I replied, "No, John summed everything up just about right." John was shocked. He was braced for an argument that never came to be. His boss politely excused me and asked John to stay. The look on both their faces revealed what was going to happen next. John implemented the changes at the staging center and the project recovered. Fortunately, John and I ended up having a good relationship and were both proud to see his tcam succeed.

Doing the right thing has always helped me achieve success, or to recover from failure, in both my personal and professional life. I highly recommend it!

Differences are Rewarding

Have you ever stopped to think about how other people see you? You may look, talk, think, or act differently. Perhaps they treat you poorly or exclude you from activities. I've been the one who was different and excluded at times, so I remember how it feels when I'm dealing with others. Instead of focusing on differences, I look for similarities and ways to include the contributions of everyone. I'm grateful for the opportunities I've had to enrich my life over the years by valuing diversity and inclusion.

My youth included several moves from city to rural, and beach to desert. Each move brought me in contact with many different people and cultures. I attended a large high school where I learned what it felt like to be a minority because there were far more people of other races than my own.

I'm a veteran of military service and I served with a wide variety of people: ex-cons, bigots, and racists, as well as some of the most dedicated, patriotic, and loving people I ever met. I lived outside the United States for several years, and I've traveled for work and pleasure. I've enjoyed learning about and working with many different people and cultures around the world.

Having adopting two children of color, I've felt their pain and witnessed their growth in spite of prejudice and bullying against them. In one instance, the middle-school band director made the mistake of bullying one of my children in front of her friends. To make a long story short, my daughter made the choice to forgive him after the school principal gave him the opportunity to apologize—in public to the entire band!

During my career, I've worked with people of many different ages, sexual orientation, and ethnic backgrounds. I've attended diversity and inclusion training, and have had both men and women managers, mentors, and coworkers. I'll never forget a coworker who eventually shared with me that he was HIV positive. I always gave him a friendly hug just as I did with anyone at work. His face always lit up with feelings of acceptance and friendship.

I once lived with a wonderful woman whose brother is gay. His partner was my hair stylist. We had many long talks about life and love while he skillfully cut my hair. We all spent time together and I came to realize that it didn't matter who was in a relationship, gay or straight, most problems and solutions were the same. Also the same is the love between two people who share their lives together.

I live in the middle of one city that is relatively poor and another that is wealthy. I've attended places of worship with several different religions, and I volunteer at a mission serving the poor. I have friends with physical disabilities, and I've experienced my own temporary disability while recovering from surgeries. If you see someone on crutches approaching a door, then please hold it open for them, thank you.

I'm now at the point in my life where I have relationships with people of all ages. I value my children and grandchildren's opinions and accomplishments, regardless of their age. I socialize with people much older and younger. My parents are now elderly, but they don't believe it yet. My family and friends have elderly siblings and parents who are dealing with economic and health issues. I'm now setting goals to be the best elderly person I can be for my family and friends in the future.

I've developed many diverse relationships over the years. I'm grateful for the positive things that have happened, and some of the negative experiences I inadvertently caused. I've learned that living a balanced life is more enjoyable, peaceful, and rewarding by valuing diversity and inclusion along the way. I hope you choose to do the same, and experience the rewards of valuing diversity and inclusion.

REFLECT ON BALANCE

Reflect on the following and discuss with *Your People:*

1. What does "live a balanced life" mean?
2. Do I live a balance life all the time?
3. What could I do to cope with an imbalanced life?
4. When is the last time I planned a vacation after I had to focus on an important project at work for a long period?
5. In what ways do I treat myself well? How do I feel when I do?
6. When dealing with other people, do I consciously think about how it feels when I treat myself well; and then use it to adjust how I treat others?
7. What image do I have of myself in terms of achieving my goals and becoming successful?
8. Do I have compassion for myself when I make mistakes?
9. What does "do the right thing" mean?
10. Who can tell me what the right thing is to do?
11. What's the difference between the Golden Rule and the Platinum Rule?
12. Who can I trust to tell me if my attitude or behavior isn't appropriate?
13. When was the last time that the right thing to do was nothing at all?
14. In what ways does doing nothing affect my health and wellbeing?
15. What is the meaning of the expression "Don't just network—build friendships and relationships?"
16. What have other people said about my interpersonal skills?
17. What is a "Captain of the World"? Do I know one? Am I one?
18. What is P.L.U.T.O. Communication and how will it help me?
19. What does "politically astute" mean?
20. How do I demonstrate that I value diversity and inclusion?

EMBRACE CHANGE	
1	**Anticipate Change**
2	The "truth" is what you perceive, not just what you hear or see
3	Be aware, informed, and open to what's possible; ask "what if?"
4	Use *Your People* to prevent scotomas and see the truth
5	**Acknowledge Change**
6	Change can be difficult and may take some time
7	You can't avoid change, it's going to happen anyway
8	*Your People* will help you acknowledge when change happens
9	**Accept Change**
10	Don't give up who you are and conform to expectations of others
11	Adapt with change and use it to accomplish your goals
12	Embrace change for success!

5. EMBRACE CHANGE

Change happens to all of us. Whether it's a change of home, job, relationship, or ourselves, change can be frightening—or exhilarating! Successful people tend not to be afraid of change. They use their Attitude of Possibility to anticipate the "thrill of the possible" in their Uncomfortable Zone. This is where they achieve break-through thinking, creativity, and innovation to accelerate their success. They've learned to embrace change because, after all, the one constant in life is that everything will change.

Nothing is permanent except change.

—*Heraclitus*

CHANGE RESULTS. "Embrace Change" means to anticipate when it's coming, know when it has occurred, then accept change by choosing to adapt with it. It's difficult to be successful by doing the same thing repeatedly while expecting different results. Embrace change for success in life!

Insanity: doing the same thing over and over again and expecting different results.

—*Albert Einstein*

CHANGE CONSTANTLY. The experts agree on the advice to embrace change. One of the most notable experts on change is Dr. Wayne Dyer. He's an international best-selling author and dubbed the "father of motivation" by his fans. In his book, *Change Your Thoughts - Change Your Life*, he describes how to apply ancient Chinese wisdom in today's modern world. Dyer notes that constant change, and the need to embrace it, is still as true today as it was back in the early centuries of humankind.

If you change the way you look at things, the things you look at change.

—*Wayne Dyer*

ANTICIPATE CHANGE

Have you ever been caught by surprise when something changed? Often it's difficult to see change coming. The RAS filters out what you're not focusing on. If you don't focus on anticipating change, then you'll never see it coming—until it's too late.

> *Sometimes we stare so long at a door that is closing that we see too late the one that is open.*
>
> *—Alexander Graham Bell*

PERCEPTION IS REALITY. **Your People** will help overcome Possibility Blockers and see the change that is coming.

> *Perception is reality, even if it's not the truth.*
>
> *—Tony Jeary*

KEY POINTS. The key points of how to anticipate change are:

- BE AWARE. Discuss current events and industry developments with other people.
- BE INFORMED. Research, analyze, identify trends, and study the competition.
- BE OPEN. Listen to loved ones at home and customers at work; they are telling you what they need. Learn what the meaning is behind their words.
- BE POSSIBLE. Ask "what if", and brainstorm possibilities. Visualize what you want to become.

ACKNOWLEDGE CHANGE

Do you know when a change has already occurred? It's difficult to acknowledge change until you admit it has happened. Our natural tendency is to avoid something we don't want to deal with. The problem with trying to avoid change is that it's going to happen anyway, with or without you.

> *It is not necessary to change. Survival is not mandatory.*
>
> *—W. Edwards Deming*

CHANGE YOUR THINKING. You may have heard the expression, "The bus is leaving the station so it's time to get on board." That is change coming. What you don't want to hear is, "The bus has already left the station so it's time to go home." One of my mentors would smile and say, "See yourself on the bus, or under it!" What about you; do you want to be on the bus, under it, or driving it? Avoiding change gives up accountability, and then other people determine your destiny. *Your People* will help you acknowledge when change has occurred. Be a victor, not a victim, and acknowledge change. Then do something about it!

> *The world as we have created it is a process of our thinking.*
> *It cannot be changed without changing our thinking.*
> —*Albert Einstein*

ACCEPT CHANGE

"Accept Change" doesn't mean giving up who you are, or conforming to the expectations of others. It means to adapt with change, and use it to accomplish goals. However, you don't have to give up core values. Core values are the fundamental beliefs about life. Use them as a guide through change. If ever unsure about accepting change, refer to your core values and make sure to stay aligned with your purpose.

> *Every human has four endowments—self-awareness, conscience, independent will and creative imagination. These give us the ultimate human freedom ... The power to choose, to respond, to change.*
> —*Stephen R. Covey*

ADAPT WITH CHANGE. It's easy to tell people that change is good and it opens up new possibilities in life. Yet it can be difficult to deal with it when it happens to you. Once you anticipate when change is coming, and acknowledge when it happens, you'll be more comfortable accepting it, and adapting with it.

> *We can't become what we need to be by remaining what we are.*
> —*Oprah Winfrey*

CHANGE WITHIN. Change is not only what happens around us, but also what happens within us. We can improve ourselves with personal development. The ability to change often as we develop our skills can result in unlimited success.

> *To improve is to change; to be perfect is to change often.*
> — *Winston Churchill*

CHANGE HAPPENS. In summary, change happens. Successful people anticipate the "thrill of the possible" in their Uncomfortable Zone. Anticipate, acknowledge, and accept change with the support of **Your People**. Embrace change as you *S.M.I.L.E. for Success*!

> *It is not the strongest of the species that survives, nor the most intelligent. It is the one that is the most adaptable to change.*
> — *Charles Galton Darwin*

STORIES ON CHANGE

The following stories are on this chapter, *Embrace Change*:

- Change Happens
- Change for Growth
- Life Lessons

Change Happens

I've had a lot of "opportunity" to learn how to embrace change over the years. My mom was married four times. She gave birth to two daughters and three sons. I never knew my father because he died in a car accident shortly before I was born. I had two different men I called "dad." I was very young when my mom divorced my first dad. My second dad is a retired Marine Corps officer, which means we moved a lot; like six or seven times, I lost count. We lived in cities, deserts, near the beach, and in mobile homes, apartments, and houses. Change happens, and a lot of it happened in my early life.

We finally settled in San Diego. I was able to complete the sixth grade through my second year of High School without moving. One day, I came home from High School and my mom sat all of us down and gave an Oscar-winning performance to announce our next move.

With a big smile she said, "It will be an adventure; so many things to do, a promotion for dad, and new friends for you kids!" In her grand finale, Mom excitedly announced, "We're moving to Barstow!" Change arrived and I never saw it coming.

The world around me slowed to a crawl as my mind raced to figure out what just happened. You've seen the movies when an explosion hits the hero, and all he hears is muted voices. Mom continued to talk, but it sounded like a Charlie Brown cartoon, "Wah, wo-wah, wa-wah." My mind began thinking with curiosity. "Let's see, I've heard of that town before. Isn't it the one on the way to Las Vegas? In the middle of the freaking desert?" Then it shifted to denial. "That's going to be a long bus ride to school. Yeah, but it will only be a couple hours more to get to the beach on the weekends." Denial turned to anger, on to bargaining, and finally stopped at depression. Accepting change wasn't going to happen this time.

Our arrival in Barstow was like a stagecoach rolling into an old western town past the tumbleweeds blowing in the wind. Could it be any hotter? People actually live here? Why is there no grass in the yard, just sand? Anyway, we had a comfortable house on the military base and I got my own room. Okay, things looked better already from my own room! My attitude improved from an impossible darkness to a manageable funk. At least I had my own private space to sulk in, probably forever. Change happened, and it almost defeated me.

It seemed like I hid in my room for several months before I started to come out of my funk. Moving while in the middle of High School just plain sucks. I vowed to never to that to my children in the future. Friends came easier than I thought and the classes were far less demanding that what I had before. I finally acknowledged that a change happened. Now it was time to do something about it. Make change happen for myself!

I went from just another trumpet player at my old school to first chair, then drum major. You've seen a drum major; that's the guy in the white uniform wearing a tall hat with a long feather. He blows the whistle and leads the marching band marking time with a majestic mace. The best part of being the drum major is that many girls love a guy in uniform. Things were changing for the better!

My mom made me take typing class, which I thought I would hate, but it turned out great because it had the prettiest girls in school. By the way, I have to thank my mom because at the time I had no idea how useful typing skills would be to my future. Sometimes, Mom really does know best!

I joined the French club (more pretty girls), volunteered on the yearbook publishing team, and my friends elected me to student government. Eventually, I became Senior Class President. I finally accepted the change of moving from the beach to the desert—in the middle of High School.

The experiences I had in youth turned out to be a great way of learning how to deal with change in the future. As it turns out, the ability to embrace change was the key to advancing my career. The lesson here is to S.M.I.L.E. and Embrace Change, because change happens!

Change for Growth

Kathy is the office manager for a well-known Orthodontic practice, and shares her life with her husband and their six children. Although she didn't set many goals in her life, Kathy managed to embrace change and used it for her benefit. The changes she experienced over the years contributed to her growth, both personally and professionally. Here is her story.

"I was born and raised in NYC. My parents are German immigrants and I'm the oldest of three children. When I was a teenager, our father moved with his job to Calgary, Alberta Canada. Overnight, the family was transported from a big bustling city to what seemed like a frozen wasteland. My ability to embrace change just began.

After adapting to my home, I graduated High School then decided to become a Registered Dental Assistant (RDA). I completed trade school and went to work for an Orthodontist whom I adored. Change was working in my favor.

My boyfriend became my husband and he was struggling to stay employed. Unknown to me, he was struggling for sanity as well, eventually being diagnosed as bi-polar. He had many grandiose plans over the years, the first moving to California for steady work. I had no problem getting a job for an Ortho practice there, but my husband's problems with work and sanity continued. I certainly didn't choose the changes with my husband and its impact on our marriage, but I continued to adapt.

Part of my training on the new job included helping at the front desk occasionally. I couldn't imagine doing that job. I had no problem talking with patients about their treatment, but talking about money was terrifying. Then another change happened. I suffered a back injury and couldn't bend over to treat patients. Sucking it up, I moved to the front desk fulltime. As a person who embraces change, I learned all the front desk jobs, figured out the new computer system, and reorganized the entire office process. I was in my Comfort Zone and loving it!

Meanwhile, more change was coming. The office manager left and a new one was hired. She became the biggest gossip in the office and eventually became a powerful Negative Wizard. She made the entire staff feel bad about themselves, especially me who had to work next to her each day. Fortunately, the Doctor was an even more Positive Wizard so I remained in my job. Suddenly, the manager abandoned me at work, and my husband abandoned me at home. Now the burden fell on me to keep the office working while recovering from my divorce. Undaunted, I accepted a promotion to office manager, and inherited the dreaded task of collecting money from patients. Change was starting to speed up now as I moved into my Uncomfortable Zone.

As a mother of two, and former wife of a mentally ill husband, I developed a strong sense of empathy for other people. I also have a strong self-confidence in my abilities at home and work. Almost naturally, I used my self-confidence to conquer the fear of asking people to pay their bills. My empathy helped to figure out a win-win for both the patient and the practice. I learned that people will pay their bill, but you have to ask them with confidence and empathy. Today, I am respected at work and I've found love with my new husband. I used change for personal growth and success in both life and love.

I embraced change in several ways; adapt to moving, dealing with mental illness, RDA certification, motherhood, divorce, vanquishing Negative Wizards, promotion, self-confidence, and the ability to achieve a win-win for the patients and the practice. I used change for growth, and so can you!"

> *When people believe you care, most of them won't turn their back on you.*
>
> — *Kathy Dreher*

Life Lessons

Diane is a wife and mother of two adult children. She and her husband enjoy spending time with their five grandchildren. She has volunteered at a hospital for many years and she loves photography. She recalls the sayings from her father at a young age. Little did she know the impact her father's wisdom would have on her future. Here is her story.

"My father had several sayings while I was growing up that I heard over and over again. So many times, in fact, that I was really tired of them. The most common were 'Any job worth doing is worth doing right,' 'There is nothing as constant as change,' and, 'Be careful who you pick as friends.' As a child, I really didn't understand all of my father's wisdom; however, I have discovered that many of these 'sayings' were excellent lessons on how to live one's life.

'Any job worth doing is worth doing right.' This saying taught me several things. It taught me to keep my promises, to do any task completely, not to quit before the job was finished, and to do it right the first time. When I was selling real estate, I realized I was applying this principle to my work ethic. If I made an appointment with someone, I kept it. I worked hard once the property was in escrow to keep everyone informed, and to be sure all signatures were obtained, even if I had to drive somewhere with paperwork to get that signature.

At the beginning of each year, the office Broker would call the agents into his office individually to go over our sales goals for the year. The formula for reaching sales goals is that a certain number of escrows attained a specific dollar amount in commissions. To get that number of escrows, one had to sell a certain number of properties. To sell that many properties an agent would have to meet with a certain number of clients. To meet that many clients we would have to make a certain number of "cold calls" either by phone or door-to-door. Every year I had to explain to the Broker that I could not operate this way. He never understood that my reward (the commission) came from treating people fairly and doing my job well.

A few years after I left that office the Broker went to jail. Apparently, office records were not accurate. There had been "co-mingling of funds" concerning client's earnest money being used for office expenses. If the job was worth doing, he should have done it right.

'There is nothing as constant as change.' I struggle with this one all the time. Change requires a huge amount of flexibility in my daily living, which is still hard for me. But it is so true—the world is changing rapidly. Over my lifetime I have seen so many inventions: the microwave, cordless phones, cell phones, the computer, and remote controls for everything. The list could go on. We used to have to get up and walk across the room to change the channel on the T.V—can you imagine? Many of these are supposedly time saving and I wonder about that. Each new thing takes an instruction book on our part—especially as we get older. We were trying to hook up a DVD player (not even a blue-ray yet) and joked that we should get the 12 year old from next door to come over and help us.

Plans change, people change, laws change, requirements change, weather changes, everything changes all the time. We have to adapt to that—a lesson I am still learning. Change came when our sons reached the age of leaving home. That was a huge change for me. Recently I became a Grandmother—WOW. Then I quit coloring my hair and it is now 'salt and pepper'. Not that long ago I was a teenager enjoying life without a care in the world, except for the atom bomb. We even had drills at school when we would take refuge under our desks, as if that would save us from the devastation of an atom bomb. Now it is terrorists to fear.

I remember the first appearance on TV by Elvis Presley and my parents would not let me watch it—said he was setting a bad example for teenagers by shaking his hips. Ha! If they could only see Miley Cyrus now! I shudder to think what my father would say. Yes, the world changes all the time, a constant change.

'Be careful who you pick as friends.' I realized by High School that my Father was teaching me to be careful whom I hung around with and be careful whom I aligned myself with. It became really clear when my own two sons were growing up. I don't think I ever used these exact words with them, but I did try and teach them that they would be judged by those around them and, so, be careful who you choose to be your friends. It was so tempting for them to go along with the crowd, for all of us really. This doesn't mean that they could not be a good example to a friend who might be headed in the wrong direction, just don't go that direction with him. This also applied to the work environment. If the company is not doing things legally (such as the real estate Broker) could I be liable in any way?

I guess my father knew what he was talking about all along. Funny how we think our parents are not real smart when we are young. The older I got the smarter my father was. I hope I've given my sons the life lessons to feel the same about me."

My father's sayings turned out to be lessons for life worth knowing.

—Diane Mount

REFLECT ON CHANGE

Reflect on the following and discuss with *Your People:*

1. What changes have I experienced that had a significant impact on my life?
2. What does "embrace change" mean?
3. What are the advantages of embracing change?
4. When was the last time I was caught by surprise when something changed?
5. Why is it difficult sometimes for me to anticipate change?
6. What can I do to anticipate change in the future?
7. How well do I know when a change has already occurred?
8. What does "accept change" mean?
9. Why should I change if I'm perfectly happy the way I am now?
10. How will embracing change help my chances for success?

S.M.I.L.E. MENTORING	
1	**What is a Mentor?**
2	You may have several short and long term coaches and mentors
3	A coach supports you in learning a skill
4	A mentor imparts wisdom and shares knowledge
5	A role model is "aspirational", a mentor is "operational"
6	Choose mentors for different areas; career, family, personal
7	**Who is Mentoring You?**
8	A mentor will help you learn to do things, but not do them for you
9	Choose mentors who will involve and inspire you
10	**Who are You Mentoring?**
11	Be a Positive Wizard to others with your actions and behavior
12	Invest in yourself; you may learn as much as you teach

6. S.M.I.L.E. Mentoring

The theme for this book is in its title …*With the Support of* **Your People**. There are many fine books on how to be successful. What makes this book different is the emphasis on **Your People**. One of **Your People** who can help achieve success faster and with fewer mistakes is a mentor.

> *Mentoring is a brain to pick, an ear to listen, and a push in the right direction.*
>
> —*John Crosby*

NEW GENERATIONS. I predict that mentoring programs will soon have a comeback as the global workforce changes generations. Whether a veteran sharing your knowledge and wisdom, or the current generation sharing new ideas and technology, *S.M.I.L.E. for Success* is a guide to help each other mange through the change.

> *No one lives long enough to learn everything they need to learn starting from scratch. To be successful, we absolutely, positively have to find people who have already paid the price to learn the things that we need to learn to achieve our goals.*
>
> —*Brian Tracy*

WHAT IS A MENTOR?

You may choose several coaches and mentors to help achieve goals. They enhance knowledge and skills, and they help you develop in different areas of life. However, there are differences between coaches and mentors, just as there are different needs for goals.

> *Learn from the experts. Study successful men and women and do what they do and you'll be successful too.*
>
> —*Brian Tracy*

COACHES. A coach is someone who provides support while you learn to achieve a specific goal. A coach is task focused. The task is well defined with the requisite steps and criteria for success. A coach helps you develop the attitude, behavior, and skills needed to perform the task successfully.

> *A coach is someone who tells you what you don't want to hear, who has you see what you don't want to see, so you can be who you have always known you could be*
>
> — Tom Landry

MENTORS. A mentor is someone who imparts wisdom and shares knowledge. Typically, mentors are more experienced in your field. They help and support by sharing their successes and lessons learned. A mentor is relationship focused. The relationship is more about personal philosophy and development rather than completing tasks.

> *True mentoring is more than just answering occasional questions or providing ad hoc help. It is about an ongoing relationship of learning, dialog, and challenge.*
>
> — Wikipedia on Mentorship

ROLE MODELS. A mentor is not necessarily a role model. A role model is an "aspirational" influence; someone you aspire to be like and want to imitate their behavior.

> *If you can't find a good role model, be one.*
>
> — Gale Anne Hurd

RELATIONSHIPS. In contrast, a mentor is an "operational" influence. You build a relationship and, over time, the mentor becomes a trusted advisor. In their book *The Trusted Advisor*, management consultants Maister, Green, and Galford define a trusted advisor as someone who values the relationship over the outcome, without any guarantee of return. Choose a mentor who is helpful and who values the relationship as much as you do.

> *It's not enough…to be right: An advisor's job is to be helpful.*
>
> — Maister, Green, and Galford

MANY CHOICES. Choose different coaches and mentors for different areas of life: career, family, and personal. A long-term coach may help develop skills in a hobby or sport. A short-term mentor may help you get through a difficult time at home or work. Seek out both long-term and short-term coaches and mentors throughout life.

> *A life is not important except in the impact it has on other lives.*
>
> *—Jackie Robinson*

	HOW TO CHOOSE A MENTOR
1	**Find Someone With More Experience**
2	A live person, older or younger, use e-mentoring if necessary
3	Don't ask, "Will you be my mentor?" It sounds like more work
4	Don't ask, "What can I do for you?" Offer to help them instead
5	Assist with something to spend more time with them
6	**Help Without Expecting Anything In Return**
7	Offer a ride to/from the airport
8	If they ask a question online, respond with a thorough write up
9	Volunteer to help with a project that they are leading
10	Do research for an article or book that they are writing
11	Help with data entry in their office
12	**Start with, "May I ask you a couple of questions?"**

HOW TO CHOOSE A MENTOR

SAME FIELD. Find someone with more experience in your field. Many schools and organizations have formal mentoring programs that can help find a more experienced mentor faster.

> *I'm not the smartest fellow in the world, but I can sure pick smart colleagues.*
>
> *—Franklin D. Roosevelt*

DIFFERENT FIELD. Alternately, find someone with more experience in another field. Sometimes a person doesn't work in the same field, but has a broader picture of what you do. I work in computers, but I've received inspiration from many other fields: airlines, hotels, insurance, restaurants, and even theme parks! The fields are different, but the principles for success are the same.

> *Experience suggests it doesn't matter so much how you got here, as what you do after you arrive.*
>
> —Lois McMaster Bujold

DIFFERENT AGE. Consider a younger mentor. A younger mentor can offer experience and guidance in new culture and technology. I love asking my children and grandchildren for help with social media. They really feel good about knowing something I don't! More importantly, it creates those magical moments with a loved one they can't get from social media. The same applies at your workplace. Try asking a younger person at work to help with a technology question. Use this as the start of a conversation that could lead to a mentoring relationship.

> *How far you go in life depends on your being tender with the young, compassionate with the aged, sympathetic with the striving and tolerant of the weak and strong. Because someday in your life you will have been all of these.*
>
> —George Washington Carver

IN PERSON. Choose a live person as a mentor. There is nothing wrong with mentoring from many sources: blogs, podcasts, books, e-books, courses, conferences, and membership sites. However, a one-on-one conversation with a person is usually much more effective, and with better results for success.

> *Many believe effective networking is done face-to-face, building a rapport with someone by looking at them in the eye, leading to a solid connection and foundational trust.*
>
> —Raymond Arroyo

Remote Mentoring. If you cannot meet with a mentor in person, then consider e-mentoring. Many forms of electronic communication can facilitate long distance mentoring: telephone, email, web-based software, and video chat services. In his book, *Everyone Needs a Mentor: Fostering Talent in Your Organisation*, global mentoring authority David Clutterbuck writes that there are advantages and disadvantages of mentoring at a distance. A key advantage is the immediacy of e-mentoring versus trying to schedule a meeting in person. The disadvantages are the potential misunderstandings from written communication and the lack of human interaction in real time. Clutterbuck's summary matches my experience that e-mentoring can be effective and, in some cases, even more effective than traditional mentoring. Sometimes people get along better remotely than in person. I wholeheartedly agree with his conclusion that the first step in mentoring is to develop a good rapport with your mentee.

> *E-mentoring is not an inferior substitute for 'real' mentoring. Rather, it is simply a different approach to mentoring and can be as effective—and in some cases, potentially more effective—than traditional approaches.*
>
> —*David Clutterbuck*

Choose a Mentor. To sum it up, choosing a mentor is an important decision that could have a great impact on success. You may have several mentors: in your field, in other fields, more or less experienced, and older or younger. Regardless of who you choose, get to know the person and develop a good rapport. If the mentor is a good fit for you, then the relationship will grow.

> *A mentor is someone who allows you to see the hope inside yourself.*
>
> —*Oprah Winfrey*

KEY POINTS. Creative ways to find and choose a mentor are:

1. Don't ask, "Will you be my mentor?"
    a. With no limits defined, imagination sets in.
    b. It sounds like way too much work.
    c. It may come off as stiff and off-putting.
2. Don't ask, "What can I do for you?"
    a. It's more work to tell you what to do.
    b. They will appreciate the initiative if you offer do to something without being asked.
3. Assist with something to spend more time with them.
    a. Offer a ride from/to the airport.
    b. Do research for their book or blog.
    c. Do data entry in their office.
4. Help without expecting anything in return.
    a. If they post a question on social media, respond with a thorough write up.
    b. Volunteer to help with a project they are leading.
    c. Offer to help recruit new staffing for their business.
5. When you have a mentor candidate in mind, try the following approaches:
    a. Invite the person out to a public place for coffee or tea.
    b. Start with, "May I ask you a couple of questions?"
    c. If this mentor candidate likes you, they'll be open to meeting or answering questions.

Who is Mentoring You?

LEAD YOU. A good mentor will help you learn to do things, but not do them for you. A mentor leads by example.

> *If your actions inspire others to dream more, learn more, do more and become more, you are a leader.*
>
> —*John Quincy Adams*

INVOLVE YOU. Choose mentors who will involve you. Most of us learn better by actually doing something rather than just hearing how to do it.

> *Tell me and I forget, teach me and I may remember, involve me and I learn.*
>
> —*Benjamin Franklin*

INSPIRE YOU. Great mentors will inspire you. My best achievements have come by learning from people who make me want to strive to be the best I can be.

> *The mediocre teacher tells. The good teacher explains. The superior teacher demonstrates. The great teacher inspires.*
>
> —*William Arthur Ward*

Who are You Mentoring?

LEARN MORE. Invest in yourself by mentoring others. Often you will learn as much, if not more, than the knowledge and wisdom imparted to other people.

> *No one learns as much about a subject as one who is forced to teach it.*
>
> —*Peter F. Drucker*

INTENTIONALLY. Sometimes, you're a mentor whether you realize it or not. People may look up to you, even if not their mentor. Attitude and behavior can be an influence on others, positive or negative. Be a Positive Wizard and a positive influence on others!

> *You don't have to be a 'person of influence' to be influential.*
> *In fact, the most influential people in my life are probably not*
> *even aware of the things they've taught me.*
>
> — *Scott Adams*

HOW TO BE A MENTOR	
1	A M.E.N.T.O.R. is:
2	**M**otivated; requires a genuine desire to help
3	**E**ncouraging; inspires hope, courage, and confidence
4	**N**urturing; teach don't tell, help grow and develop
5	**T**imely; stay focused, respect each other's time
6	**O**ptimistic; don't give up, be positive and patient
7	**R**espectful; listen, don't lecture, give constructive feedback
8	**Get to Know a Mentee by Asking:**
9	"What is it that you really want to be and do?"
10	"What should you **start** doing that will help you get there?"
11	"What should you **stop** doing that is preventing you?"
12	"What should you **continue** doing that is helping you?"

HOW TO BE A MENTOR

RAPPORT. The first step in being a mentor is to develop a good rapport with your mentee. As a mentor, get to know a mentee by asking these open-ended questions:

1. What is it that you really want to be and do?
2. What should you **start** doing that will help you get there?
3. What should you **stop** doing that is preventing you from getting there?
4. What should you **continue** doing that is helping you get there?
5. Where do you need the most help?
6. How can I help?

REWARDS. The rewards of being a mentor include enhanced leadership skills, learning from the emerging talent pool, growing your career network, and the satisfaction of giving back to the organization or profession.

I mentor others the way I would want to be mentored.
—Variation of the Golden Rule

KEY POINTS. The acronym "M.E.N.T.O.R." summarizes how to be a mentor:

- **M**otivated
    - Being a mentor is hard work.
    - It requires a genuine desire to help.

- **E**ncouraging
    - Inspire hope, courage, and confidence.
    - Be a role model and lead by example.
    - Have fun!

- **N**urturing
    - Teach don't tell.
    - Help grow and develop.
    - Be open-minded and compassionate.

- **T**imely
    - Stay focused.
    - Make a schedule and respect each other's time.

- **O**ptimistic
    - Don't give up.
    - Be positive and patient.
    - Expect a favorable outcome.

- **R**espectful
    - Give constructive feedback.
    - Be curious, not critical, or judgmental.
    - Share the conversation rather than doing all the talking.
    - Don't interrupt unless you need to manage the time.

	HOW TO BE A MENTEE
1	**A M.E.N.T.E.E. is:**
2	**M**otivated; requires a genuine desire to learn and grow
3	**E**ncouraging; be open, honest and real in your communication
4	**N**urturing; acknowledge opportunities for development
5	**T**imely; stay focused, respect each other's time
6	**E**arnest; don't give up, be positive and patient
7	**E**ngaging; be appreciative and say, "Thank you!"
8	**Get to Know a Mentor by Asking:**
9	"What would you answer if asked what do you do for a living?"
10	"Describe a typical day at your job?"
11	"How did you end up doing the job you have today?"
12	"What education and training have you had to get your job?"

HOW TO BE A MENTEE

RAPPORT. The first step in being a mentee is to develop a good rapport with your mentor. Get to know a mentor by asking the following open-ended questions. Be prepared with answers if asked these same questions by your mentor:

1. What would you answer if someone asked, "what do you do for a living?"
2. Describe a typical day at your job?
3. How did you end up doing the job you have today?
4. What education and training have you had to get your job?
5. How do you define success?
6. Where do you see yourself in five years?

REWARDS. The rewards of being a mentee include enhanced skills, learning from experience, growing your career network, and the satisfaction of personal and professional growth.

> *One of the great keys to success is to use proven success methods. Learn from the experts; don't try to re-invent the wheel. Life is too short for that.*
>
> —*Brian Tracy*

KEY POINTS. The acronym "M.E.N.T.E.E." summarizes how to be a mentee:

- **M**otivated
    - Being a mentee is hard work.
    - It requires a genuine desire to learn and grow.

- **E**ncouraging
    - Be willing to learn from the experience of others.
    - Be open, honest, and real in communication.
    - Have fun!

- **N**urturing
    - Show the desire to learn.
    - Acknowledge opportunities for growth.
    - Be open-minded and compassionate.

- **T**imely
    - Stay focused.
    - Make a schedule and respect each other's time.

- **E**arnest
    - Don't give up.
    - Be positive and patient.
    - Expect a favorable outcome.

- **E**ngaging
    - Listen to constructive feedback regardless if you take the mentor's advice or not.
    - Be curious, not critical, or judgmental.
    - Share the conversation rather than doing all the talking.
    - Be appreciative and say, "Thank you!"

STORIES ON MENTORING

The following stories are on this chapter, *S.M.I.L.E. Mentoring*:

- Role Model and Mentor
- Go Figure
- I Matter
- My Mentors

Role Model and Mentor

Bruce is a manager for a large computer corporation who enjoys his beautiful wife, five children, and their grandchildren. Outside of work, he spends time with his family, as well as hunting, fishing, coaching basketball, and volunteering. One day something happened to Bruce that led him to discover his role model was also his mentor. Here is his story.

"I view mentors and role models similarly in some respects. Most of my mentors are role models and vice versa. With that in mind, my first and most influential mentor and role model was my father. Dad was the tenth of twelve children. He lost the lower half of his right leg in a farm accident at the age of two, and had to endure multiple surgeries and a lot of pain. He grew up on a farm and, even though he was missing a leg, he was expected to help. He was the first one in his family to graduate from high school and attended a trade school. During these years, he worked many jobs including delivery driver, laborer, and a brick layers assistant hauling brick and concrete around all day long. He also held a second job as gas station attendant and mechanic.

My father was an extremely hard and dedicated worker, and rose to the top of his job at virtually everything he did. He always strived to do his best and learn. He had been turned down for jobs in the mines because of his missing leg, eventually landing a job in a steel foundry making castings for the mining industry. He started as a mechanic and quickly rose through the ranks to become the Plant Superintendent. He oversaw every facet of the operation, and made sure everyone worked hard and did their best. He trained all of his people and helped them grow as individuals. Being in a very risky business, he demanded that everyone work safely and watched over the critical molten metal pouring process like a hawk. If there was molten metal in the plant—he was there.

Dad instilled the same kinds of drive, work ethic, hunger for knowledge, and compassion for others in each of his children. One of my more memorable learning moments was during a summer break at college. I worked as a delivery person for an oil and gas company where most of my days were spent delivering bulk oil in 55 gallon drums. I also filled in as a gas station attendant when others were on vacation.

One Friday night I was out late enjoying a little too much adult beverage, so I decided to open the gas station a little late; 8 am instead of the normal 6 am. I had done this before and my boss said it was perfectly acceptable. At 5:45 am, my father was in my room waking me and asking me, not politely, why I wasn't on my way to work. I told him I was going to open at 8:00, which my father found unacceptable even though my boss said it was okay. As he saw it, people were depending on the gas station to be open at 6 am so opening late would cost business. I wasn't going back to sleep, if I had tried he probably would have pulled me out of bed. I was at work by 6:30.

When I got home, Dad had softened a bit from the morning wake up call. He and I had a long conversation about being dependable and the value of customers. It was a lesson I have never forgotten. It's also when I made it a point never to be late again. My mantra became the same as former MLB baseball pitcher Scott Mullen, "If you're not five minutes early, you're late." In this special teaching moment, my father became both my mentor and role model."

I think the world needs role models and mentors.

—*Bruce Frericks*

Go Figure

Do you ever think twice about using a calculator to solve a math problem? When I started teaching electronics theory in the late 1970's, calculators were new and students weren't allowed to use them. The thinking at the time was that if students used calculators, then they wouldn't learn the building blocks of the subject. As a new teacher, I didn't know any better and asked in a staff meeting, "Why not?"

The focus of the entire room suddenly shifted and everyone glared at me with scornful looks as the leader challenged my competence. Instead of answering my question, he made the mistake of asking me to explain why we should allow calculators. Again, not knowing any better, I answered his question with another question, "Are we teaching electronics theory or mathematics?" We started allowing calculators shortly thereafter. It was obvious to all that the students already knew math, so using a pencil and paper was just stealing valuable time they needed to learn electronics.

Most of us today don't think twice about using a calculator. So why is it different than asking a more experienced person for their assistance? Why should you go it alone, make all the mistakes, and waste so much time not achieving goals? Why not learn from the experience of others and use the time saved to achieve success in life? Yes, you'll still make mistakes and have setbacks along the way. However, armed with the experience of others who have made the same mistakes before, you'll have more options of how to succeed.

I'll share a secret that no one told me when I first got started. People with more experience actually **want** you to ask them for help! If you follow the guidelines in this book, and add some creativity, then you may be able to develop important mentoring relationships. Relationships that could make all the difference in achieving even more success than you'd think possible—and faster!

So what does using a calculator have to do with asking for assistance? The difference, of course, is just picking up a tool versus working to build and nurture mentoring relationships. People are just harder and more complex than tools. Well, so are goals. Go figure!

I Matter

Rick is a retired police officer and lives with his fabulous wife and their two children. He enjoys family activities, boating, photography, and golf. He is active at his church and is the president of the booster club for his son's High School marching band. Rick had many assignments over the years and learned some valuable lessons along the way about mentoring. Here is his story.

"When you really enjoy your job, it's easy to lose sight of priorities at home and in your personal life. My career was with the largest sheriff's department in the country. I was a hard charging, "hooking, and booking" cop, loving the excitement of patrolling the gang-filled streets in the suburbs of a large metropolitan city. I liked working the early morning shift where the most action seemed to occur, but I was a newlywed and my wife was always concerned for my safety. This shift, while lots of fun, was not conducive to family life, especially in the beginning stages of building a family. I worked at a "fast" station and thought I was doing everything right to put myself in a position for promotion when the time would come.

A couple of years later, I transferred to a different station to be closer to home but still a one-hour commute to work. I worked as a training officer on the evening shift before moving into an undercover position. Working undercover is a position where you move when the "bad guys" move and do surveillance at all hours of the night and day. Again, I was having the time of my life doing real police work, but it was anything but conducive to married life.

Eventually I transferred to work the day shift at the Inmate Reception Center downtown with plans to have more time at home and earn a promotion to sergeant. It was a busy time and overtime was plentiful, whether we wanted it or not. My work took me away from my wife who needed a husband and my two children that needed a dad. The strain eventually gave way to a divorce, not because we stopped loving each other, but because we stopped being a family.

I promoted to the rank of sergeant and attended a mandatory school where we learned the ethics, expectations, and responsibilities that come with the sergeant position. One day, a well-respected commander on the department spoke about doing what it takes to succeed as well as balance both our professional and personal life. He handed out 3x5 index cards and asked everyone to write two goals on the card, one professional, one personal, one short-term, and one long-term. I wrote my personal and short-term goal as "remarry my ex-wife," and my professional and long-term goal as "promote to the rank of lieutenant." He told us to tuck the card away somewhere and look at it periodically as a reminder; then do what it takes to make these goals happen. Most sergeants just went through the motions and trashed the index card once the class was over. I, however, did exactly as instructed. Little did I know what impact it would have on my life!

It was at that moment that I decided to change my priorities and focus on rebuilding my relationship with my ex-wife. I made a commitment to her and myself that "family comes first." Five months later, my ex-wife and I remarried. Although being the wife of a police office is never easy, I made sure I did everything possible to take positions that afforded me the most opportunity to be a husband and a dad. That was many years ago and today we still have a strong husband/wife relationship and a loving family.

I had numerous opportunities to use my position as a sergeant to tell my personal story to young deputies. I explained how I let "the department" and the excitement of being a "street cop" take control of my life and ruin my marriage and my family. When I saw them making the same mistakes I made as a young deputy, I sat down with them over a cup of coffee and would tell my story. I know these true story chats saved dozens of marriages, and some careers along the way.

At the same time, I was also working to achieve my long-term goal of promotion to lieutenant. I took several "promotional positions" to make rank but it seemed like it would never happen. One day I was having a conversation with a department captain. I was telling him about my frustration of how long it was taking for my promotion. I pulled out a tattered and yellowing index card that I kept for more than seven years. I showed him I had reached my short-term goal of remarrying my ex-wife and was losing hope of reaching my long-term goal.

He recognized the index card was from the class his boss gave in sergeant's school. The captain suggested that I set up a career counseling session with his boss, now the Undersheriff. He said that the Undersheriff is always willing to meet with people and give suggestions on how to better their career. I scheduled the meeting with anxiety of meeting with such a high-level person.

I found myself sitting in the Undersheriff's office, more nervous than I had ever been in my career. He took the time to make me feel comfortable then gave me the opportunity to say what was on my mind. I told him that I thought I was doing everything right to put myself in a position to promote but it was taking too long. He was sincere when he said I had done everything right and had already proven myself completely worthy of promoting. He explained that I am one employee among some twenty thousand. There are over three hundred sergeants worthy of promoting to lieutenant and sometimes the good ones don't get the promotion just because there are so many qualified sergeants.

I then pulled out the same tattered and yellowing index card, showed it to him, and explained that I took his class seriously several years ago. He read, "remarry my ex-wife," and asked if I had reached that goal. I told him yes, to which he raised his hand and we did a "high five." He asked me how my marriage was going and I explained that it was going great, now that I put my family first. He smiled. I then thanked him for his time and told him I will continue to do everything I can to promote to lieutenant. We ended with a firm handshake and he thanked me for taking the time to meet with him. Three days later, my name appeared on the promotion list and I achieved my long-term goal of the rank of lieutenant.

So what does all of this mean? For me, it shows the importance of balancing family life and work life, and when the two are in conflict, family needs to win. It's about priorities, making them and holding true to them. After all, when you are done with your career, those who worked with you will eventually forget your name and new employees will never know who you were or what you did while on the job. To give up your family for that just doesn't make sense. In the end, who wants to die alone?

I learned that as we advance in our careers, we have more influence and a higher obligation to mentor those around us. We need to make an opportunity for others to better themselves by learning from our failures and successes.

In addition, I learned that we need to take what people are trying to teach us seriously and we should not shrug off a lecturer as just another "required to attend" event. Don't worry about what other people are saying or doing, and don't just go through the motions. Hang onto that tattered and yellow index card. Remember whatever someone has taken the time to teach you. You may not see the value right way. It may take years before you understand the real value of what you learned.

Finally, I learned how such a small amount of time could have such a great impact. It's not what we do in that time, but how we do it. When the Undersheriff, the second in command of the largest sheriff's department in the country, took the time make me feel comfortable, listen to what I had to say, and then personally help me make the promotion list—it mattered. I mattered!

I have taken that approach with all of my subordinates throughout my career. I went out of my way to show them they matter and they are valued. I came out from behind the desk and sat with them. I sat and chatted with them in their cubical, I often stopped what I was doing to help them, both personally and professionally. I enjoyed getting to know them as a person, not just an employee. In the end, they knew they were important to me. I had loyal staff because they knew I had their best interest in mind at all times, and I was able to balance that with the need to meet the strategic goals required of the job. I wanted them always to be able to look in the mirror and say, "I matter!"

Even a small amount of time given to someone can have a great impact.

—*Rick Meyers*

My Mentors

I am fortunate to have had several mentors in many areas of my personal and professional life. With an Attitude of Gratitude, I would like to tell you about a special few. I've kept it brief, but I hope you'll take away an idea of what mentoring is all about to me, and can be for you. Mentors can be few or many, short or long-term, known or unknown, and personal or professional. Mentors are truly **Your People**.

My mom and dad have been mentors in many different ways. Sometimes they've taught me the best way to live my life, and other times I've learned from their mistakes. Like most people, I didn't always appreciate my parents when I was young. As I grew up and became a parent, I came to understand that they always had my best interest in mind. I've inherited my mom's infectious optimism and my dad's disciplined determination. I use both to my advantage when I set goals. For that, I'll always be grateful. Thank you, Marva and Steve!

My grandparents lived in a small town known for its copper mining industry. My grandfather was a proud miner who worked hard all of his life. My grandmother took care of him and their three children: my father, aunt, and uncle. From their examples, I learned the value of hard work, setting goals, loyalty, and getting along with other people. Thank you Jesse, Orville, Bud, Linda, Jim, and Juliene!

The first mentor I had in the Army was the late Paul Bricker. Paul conquered his disability and became a great educator. I write about him in Chapter 1, *Teaching Without a Voice*. He didn't mentor me on just how to teach. By his example, I learned how to convey knowledge to others. He was so energetic and positive that his students **desired** to learn. He had no voice but many listened to what he had to say, including me. Thank you, Paul!

When I left the Army, I didn't have a job lined up and my family had nowhere to stay. Not only did Gene Low take us all in, he became a mentor without knowing it. He is an example of a loving father and husband who taught me valuable lessons the short time we lived there. I could've been a better student at the time, but I'll always be grateful to him and his family. Thank you, Gene!

I've had a few short-term mentors. I never met the late Lou Tice, but he still managed to teach me how to change my life with his training program, *Investment in Excellence*®. Another mentor was Tony Jeary. I only met Tony once yet I adopted him as a mentor and, unbeknownst to him, he inspired me to finish this book. Thank you, Lou and Tony!

Another short-term mentor I had was Alex Valladares. Alex unselfishly prepared me to pass my management board. He spent many hours during the week, at night, and on weekends drilling me with questions and scenarios. He scolded me when I needed it, and supported me through it all. He helped me achieve a very important goal in my life. Thank you, Alex!

A long-term mentor during my career was Aggie Rucker. What can I say about Aggie? I could tell you about how she taught me the value of diversity and loyalty, and what a caring person she is. And I could say that she believed in me when I needed it the most, and opened doors that I didn't know existed. Or, I could just say how much I appreciate everything she has ever done for my family and me. Thank you, Aggie!

One long-term mentor stands out from the rest. Fred Fernandez is a great leader, coach, mentor, and friend. He opened many doors for me in my career. Fred helped me through setbacks in my life, and he continues to believe in me today. His family has adopted me as one of their own. Fred is one of the most selfless people I know and a very Positive Wizard. Truly, he is one of "*My People*." Thank you, Fred!

As you can see, there are many different kinds of mentors for many different areas of life. It's no longer a secret–they really **want** to help! Now it's up to you. S.M.I.L.E. and seek out mentors that are there just waiting for you to take the first step. I hope you will, and I hope mentors become as meaningful to you as mine are to me!

Reflect on Mentoring

Reflect on the following and discuss with *Your People:*

1. What's the difference between a coach and a mentor?
2. What's the difference between a role model and a mentor?
3. Why should I choose a live person as a mentor rather than books and online blogs?
4. What are some of the creative ways I can find and choose a mentor?
5. Why should I choose mentors in my field and in other fields?
6. Is there any benefit in choosing a younger mentor?
7. What are the advantages and disadvantages of e-mentoring?
8. What do I expect a mentor to do for me?
9. In what way am I a mentor to other people?
10. What is the first step in starting a new mentoring relationship?
11. What is a M.E.N.T.O.R.?
12. What are the rewards of being a mentor?
13. What is a M.E.N.T.E.E.?
14. What are the rewards of being a mentee?
15. How can mentoring help me become successful faster and with fewer failures?

S.M.I.L.E. CONTINUOUSLY	
1	**S.M.I.L.E. is Action**
2	Success requires action, so what are you waiting for?
3	You cannot wait until completely ready, it will always be too late
4	Achieving goals builds confidence
5	**S.M.I.L.E. is Ageless**
6	You are never too old, or too young, to start living intentionally
7	Manage goals for all stages of your life:
8	School, college, job, career, retirement, elderly, death, legacy
9	**S.M.I.L.E. is Continuous**
10	Success is not a one-time event, and neither is managing goals
11	Don't flatten out; set the next goal before achieving the current one
12	Continuously set goals, prevail over setbacks, celebrate success!

7. S.M.I.L.E. Continuously

We all have things we want to do or become. Our wants change over time as we grow and as the world changes around us. We get what we want by setting goals. We don't just set goals one time; we set them continuously. Therefore, S.M.I.L.E. is a continuous process designed to achieve success throughout our lives.

> *The only path to ultimate lifelong success is daily consistent action towards your life's purpose!*
>
> — *Tony Robbins*

REPETITION. Repetition is the key to retaining what you learn and changing behavior. Refer back to this book frequently, and reflect on the questions at the end of each chapter. Review the note cards in each section with **Your People** to sustain motivation for success!

> *People often say that motivation doesn't last. Well, neither does bathing. That's why we recommend it daily.*
>
> — *Zig Ziglar*

S.M.I.L.E. is Action

Everything you do is a choice. Success is taking responsibility for choices, being empowered to take action, and accountable for the results. If you really want success, then the only choice is to take action—so what are you waiting for?

> *Everything you want is out there waiting for you to ask. Everything you want also wants you. But you have to take action to get it.*
>
> — *Jules Renard*

TAKE ACTION. Most of us like to be fully prepared, but sometimes we over prepare and miss opportunities for success. For example, we prepare to go to work by looking for our smartphone and wallet. If we over prepare by stopping to update our apps and organize our wallet every time we leave for work, then we would be late and suffer the consequences. You cannot wait until completely ready; it will always be too late!

> *Create a definite plan for carrying out your desire and begin at once, whether you ready or not, to put this plan into action.*
>
> *—Napoleon Hill*

START SMALL. Wanting something without taking action is self-defeating. It's never going to happen and you'll resent not even trying to get it. But it doesn't have to be that way! Start with a small goal, involve **Your People**, finish it, and celebrate a small success. Then set another goal a little higher. Keep doing this and soon you'll realize how capable and powerful you are to accomplish goals. Achieving goals builds confidence and leads to even more success!

> *Action is a great restorer and builder of confidence. Inaction is not only the result, but the cause, of fear. Perhaps the action you take will be successful; perhaps different action or adjustments will have to follow. But any action is better than no action at all.*
>
> *—Norman Vincent Peale*

GET STARTED. S.M.I.L.E. is an acronym of action words: Select, Manage, Invest, Live, and Embrace. It's never too late; it's always the right time to take action for success. You'll never be completely prepared, but always ready enough. S.M.I.L.E. is action, so "ready-fire-aim" and get started today!

> *Ready, fire, aim.*
>
> *—Michael Landon*

S.M.I.L.E. IS AGELESS

People of most ages and backgrounds will understand the plain language used in this book. When children start to ask questions on how to get what they want, then parents may choose to introduce S.M.I.L.E. to them. Start with small topics over time rather than the entire book at once. Young adults from their teens through college would especially benefit from this book. They are on the cusp of figuring out what they want to do or become. They tend to be more open to change and trying new things. Working adults have many goals to achieve as they advance through their career. Older adults have goals for retirement and their post-retirement years. You are never too young, too old, or too experienced to start setting goals and living life intentionally.

> *You are never too old to set another goal or to dream a new dream.*
>
> —*C. S. Lewis*

LIVE LONGER. The one constant in life is change. Well, so is getting older. We're all going to do it, we're never fully prepared, and it can be scary. Why not plan to grow old **before** it happens? In their famous book, *The Longevity Project*, Dr. Howard Friedman and Dr. Leslie Martin spent eight decades collecting an enormous amount of data on health and longevity. Their research indicates that most people have a more enjoyable life and tend to live longer when they feel like they are in control of their own destiny.

> *You always hear advice to take it easy and not work so hard but this turned out to be wrong, wrong, wrong! Hard work was not a health problem. Contrary to what most people think, it was the happy-go-lucky, less successful folks who were at greatest risk of dying.*
>
> —*Dr. Howard Friedman*

ALL STAGES. Be in control of your destiny and live a longer and more enjoyable life! Manage goals to do or become whatever you choose through all stages of life:

- School / College
- Job / Career
- Retirement / Elderly
- Death / Legacy

ALL AGES. Regardless of background and experience, you can *S.M.I.L.E. for Success* at any age!

> *We come altogether fresh and raw into the several stages of life, and often find ourselves without experience, despite our years.*
>
> —*Francois de La Rochefoucauld*

S.M.I.L.E. IS CONTINUOUS

Success is not a one-time event in life, and neither is managing goals. Just as our lives are continuous, so is the pursuit of our purpose. We'll have setbacks and successes along the way. S.M.I.L.E. helps us prevail over setbacks and celebrate successes with enthusiasm.

> *Success consists of going from failure to failure without loss of enthusiasm.*
>
> —*Winston Churchill*

REALIZE GOALS. S.M.I.L.E. continuously: set goals, prevail over setbacks, and celebrate success!

> *Success is the progressive realization of predetermined, worthwhile, personal goals.*
>
> —*Paul J. Meyer*

KEEP GOING. S.M.I.L.E. and complete the goals that achieve your purpose. To avoid flattening out, set the next goal before finishing the current one.

> *Your goals are the road maps that guide you and show you what is possible for your life.*
>
> —*Les Brown*

ENJOY THE JOURNEY. *S.M.I.L.E. for Success* is continuous action at any age throughout life. Select Your Attitude, Manage Your Goals, Invest in Yourself, Live a Balanced Life, and Embrace Change. Do this continuously and achieve more success than you thought was possible. Remember, success in a journey. Enjoy your journey!

S.M.I.L.E. for Success, With the Support of Your People!

Reflect on S.M.I.L.E.

Reflect on the following and discuss with *Your People:*

1. What does Select Your Attitude mean?
    a. Is everything **really** a choice, and why?
    b. What do all these attitudes mean: Choice, Accountability, Gratitude, Possibility, and Purpose?
    c. What can each of these attitudes do for me?
    d. In what ways do I select my attitude for positive results?
    e. When have I had a negative attitude and what did I do about it?
    f. How would I advise others to select their attitude and why?
    g. What are examples of how I live in the Possibility Zone with affirmations and visualization?
    h. What is the Reticular Activating System and why is it important to me?
    i. Am I a Positive Wizard to others and myself?
    j. Am I a Possibility Wizard?
    k. What areas of improvement do I have for selecting my attitude?

2. What does Manage Your Goals mean?
    a. Do I know what my purpose is?
    b. How well do I manage my goals to achieve my purpose?
    c. What would I advise others on managing their goals?
    d. What areas of improvement do I have for managing my goals?

3. What does Invest in Yourself mean?
    a. Does my appearance help or hurt my opportunities for success?
    b. How have I invested in myself and what were the results?
    c. What areas of improvement do I have in providing Added Value Support?
    d. Can I recite my elevator pitch in under one minute?
    e. What areas of improvement do I have for investing in myself?

4. What does Live a Balanced Life mean?

   a. What is the image I have of myself?

   b. Am I compassionate with others and myself?

   c. What does "Do the Right Thing" mean?

   d. What areas of improvement do I have in resolving conflict?

   e. How well do I build relationships?

   f. What areas of improvement do I have for living a balanced life?

5. What does Embrace Change mean?

   a. What does "anticipate, acknowledge, and accept change" mean?

   b. What are examples of how I've embraced changed with positive results?

   c. What areas of improvement do I have for embracing change?

6. What is S.M.I.L.E. Mentoring?

   a. What is a mentor and how do I choose one?

   b. What can a mentor do for me?

   c. What would it mean to others for me to be their mentor?

   d. What areas of improvement do I have for mentoring?

7. What does S.M.I.L.E. Continuously mean?

   a. Why do I have to take action to achieve my goals?

   b. What would it take to start setting goals and involving others in my success?

   c. What would it take to help others start setting their own goals?

   d. Is there anything preventing me from taking action to be in control of my own destiny?

   e. What areas of improvement do I have to S.M.I.L.E. continuously?

APPENDIX

GOAL SHEET EXAMPLE

Goals and objectives are written as affirmations—in the present tense as if they've already been achieved. S.M.A.R.T. criteria is:

1. SPECIFIC
   a. Clear and unambiguous.
   b. Answer the five W's: Who, What, When, Where, Why?
2. MEASURABLE
   a. Objective criteria (facts), versus subjective (opinions).
   b. How many, how long, what standards for quality?
3. ACHIEVABLE
   a. Realistic and attainable.
   b. Is it achievable within the timeframe specified?
4. RELEVANT
   a. Goals that matter to you and others.
   b. Do I really need this?
5. TIME-BOUND
   a. Target milestones and dates for completion.
   b. What is the schedule and due date?

S.	M.	A.	R.	T.
I'm a published author	My book and eBook is available online	I have the ambition, skills, and support	Career, Personal	June 2014
We are enjoying our vacation at a beach resort	We are relaxing on the beach enjoying the warm sun	Our financial goals are on track, no stress over the budget	Family, Personal	Annually
I have reduced my weight by 12%	I'm on the digital scale and see the display	I have the attitude, resources, and support I need	Career, Family, Personal	6 Months
I have been promoted to a Master Level Business Consultant	I'm reading the recognition email	I have a mentor and the support of management, both confirm I'm ready	Career, Personal	Q2 FY14

STATUS REPORT EXAMPLE

Reporting status and results is not the time to be bashful! Select an Attitude of Accountability and be empowered to accept the consequences. Remember, success is a consequence—a positive one!

The key points of producing a report to the boss are:

- EXECUTIVE SUMMARY. This is your first impression so make it a good one! The boss has a lot to read so get to the point fast and keep it concise. Clearly state the objectives, what you need to be successful, and a concise bottom-line status.

- PROJECT STATUS. List the accomplishments to goals: progress to schedule, cost to budget, and quality to standards.

- NEXT STEPS. List the key accomplishments planned for the next reporting period.

- RISK PLAN. List the key risks and risk management plans.

- REWARDS AND RECOGNITION. Take the time to acknowledge individual and team contributions. Your boss will appreciate this, and it's a strong motivator to most employees.

- COMMENTARY AND CONCLUSION. This is your opportunity to show critical thinking skills as well as an Attitude of Possibility.

All of the key points come together in the following example that can be modified for your own use:

STATUS REPORT FOR: Employee Training Project

EXECUTIVE SUMMARY

FYI only: There is no action for management at this time. We are on schedule and under budget, but the status is "YELLOW" due to a training supplier who couldn't deliver on time. An alternate supplier is on board and we expect a status of "GREEN" for the next report.

PROJECT STATUS

GOAL #1: Develop employee skills.

STATUS: Supplier 'A' couldn't deliver on time so we hired supplier 'B' as a replacement. This put us 2 weeks behind schedule and 10% over budget as the new supplier is more expensive. However, we can make up the budget with a faster training schedule in the contract with the new supplier.

NEXT STEPS

1. Conduct training through Q1.
2. Monitor employee satisfaction quarterly.
3. Monitor customer satisfaction with annual survey.

RISK PLAN

1. There is a risk the new supplier cannot deliver on schedule, resulting in a cost overrun to the budget. We have transferred this risk to the supplier with a performance penalty if they fail to meet the schedule, and a reward of new business next year if they complete the training as promised.

REWARDS AND RECOGNITION

1. Mary in procurement scored a huge win for the project by negotiating a win-win contract with the new supplier. Thank you, Mary!
2. Tom received an employee recognition reward for his contribution to collaborating with all business groups to modify the training schedule. Great job, Tom!

COMMENTARY AND CONCLUSION

The team is working well together and spirits are high. The decision to change training suppliers in the early stages of the project was not made lightly. We collaborated with the company's procurement organization and completed a Pareto analysis of options and risks to come to the decision that it was the best course of action. In conclusion, we are committed to achieving our objectives and we are on track.

SELF-MANAGEMENT TIPS

Self-management refers to the tools and techniques used to direct your actions toward achieving goals. The key areas of self-management are Critical Thinking, Organization, and Time Management.

Critical Thinking

Critical thinking is determining truth or fiction, right or wrong, good or bad, and cause and effect. Critical in this context doesn't mean disapproval. It means to think about truth, merit, and logical conclusion.

People use critical thinking skills to make decisions and solve problems. In short: identify the problem, brainstorm options for resolution, prioritize the list, recommend solutions, get acceptance, and implement the plan.

The acronym "T.R.U.E." is a summary of the critical thinking process: Truth, Reality, Unexpected, and Effect.

- TRUTH. Truth is what we perceive: our opinion of the truth based on beliefs and values.

- REALITY. Reality is the truth based on facts and evidence.

- UNEXPECTED. Brainstorm to see truth and reality that is alternate, hidden, opposite, and unexpected.

- EFFECT. Most everything has a cause and effect. The effect is the logical conclusion, or the obvious outcome. For example, if you repeatedly show up for work late, you'll eventually have to find another job.

Organization

Organization skills are crucial to keep up in this fast-paced world. If you miss appointments or deadlines, and can't seem to get caught up with your workload, then you'll benefit by improving how you organize your life. Involve **Your People** to help improve organization skills and increase opportunities for success!

The acronym "S.P.E.E.D." is a summary of organization skills: Schedule, Paper, Email, Efficiency, and Desk.

- SCHEDULE. Use an online calendar and synchronize with your computers and smartphone.

- PAPER. Have a one-touch approach to organizing paper. Read then file, shred, or trash. The only paper on your desk should be what you're working on today. File unfished work at the end of the day. Schedule one day per year to purge paper files.

- EMAIL. Read then file or delete. With modern email applications and spacious storage devices, you can file all the email for a year in one folder. Save each email with a key word in the subject field. Use the search feature to find email with the key word. Start a new folder each year and purge the old folders after a reasonable amount of time.

- EFFICIENCY. When starting a new task, invest time to figure out how to do it better/cheaper/faster in the future. Use this repeatable process the next time you do the same task. You'll finish it faster, making time to learn new skills and complete more tasks.

- DESK. Your personal workspace is on your computer, smartphone, and desk. Handle electronic documents the same as paper: read, file, or delete. Schedule one day per year to purge electronic files. Your workspace reflects your personality and work style. However it's organized, make sure it's as efficient as possible to help achieve goals for success.

Time Management

The most important self-management skill is time management. Time is precious, limited, and irreplaceable. Manage it well.

The acronym "T.I.M.E." is a summary of time management skills: To-do list, Interruptions, Meetings, E-messaging.

- TO-DO LIST. Create a "TO-DO" entry on your office suite calendar with a reminder at the start of each workday. List your top 10 tasks, prioritize the list, and focus on the top 3. Update the TO-DO entry as your tasks and priorities change. Keep it simple. Many successful people manage their to-do list with a pad of paper and pencil.

- INTERRUPTIONS. Manage interruptions by scheduling "available" and "unavailable" time on your calendar. If interrupted with a new task request, then say "yes" instead of "no." For example, "Yes, and when do you need it?" Or, "Yes, and what priority can we change?" Successful people learn to limit interruptions, focus on the task, and achieve their goals.

- MEETINGS. Select an Attitude of Accountability and only attend necessary meetings. Proactively work with the meeting scheduler to define the agenda and timeline.

- E-MESSAGING. E-messaging includes email, text messages, and social media. Don't feel you have to reply to e-messages immediately. Reply only if necessary. The ability to manage e-messaging is crucial for effective time management.

Reflect on Self-Management

Reflect on the following and discuss with *Your People*.

Reflect on T.R.U.E. critical thinking:
1. "Is the issue a perception of the truth?"
2. "Is it reality based on evidence and facts?"
3. "What is the alternate, hidden, opposite, and unexpected?"
4. "If true/false, what is the logical conclusion?

Reflect on S.P.E.E.D. organization:
1. "Is my online schedule sync'd with my smartphone and PC?"
2. "Do I touch paper only one time?"
3. "Do I read email then file or delete it?"
4. "How can I do it better/cheaper/faster?"
5. "Is my desk organized as efficiently as possible?"
6. "What can I do to S.P.E.E.D. achievement of my goals?"

Reflect on T.I.M.E. management:
1. "What's the best use of my T.I.M.E. right now?"
2. "Yes, and when do you need it?"
3. "Yes, and what priority can we change?"
4. "Is this meeting necessary?"
5. "Can I respond to this e-message later, tomorrow, next week, or never?"

QR CODE INDEX

For further information about the topics below, scan the QR Codes with your smartphone app.

SELECT YOUR ATTITUDE

MANAGE YOUR GOALS

INVEST IN YOURSELF

LIVE A BALANCED LIFE

EMBRACE CHANGE

S.M.I.L.E. MENTORING

S.M.I.L.E. CONTINUOUSLY

BIBLIOGRAPHY

Alessandra, Tony. The Platinum Rule: Discover the Four Basic Business Personalities and How They Can Lead You to Success. New York City: Warner Business Books, 1998. (Platinum Rule)

Aristotle. Explanation and Teleology in Aristotle's Science of Nature. Mariska Leunissen (Author). Cambridge Press, 2010. (The teleological nature of humans)

Blair, Gary Ryan. Goal Setting 101: How to Set and Achieve a Goal! Blair Pub House, 2000. (Manage Your Resources)

Breines, Juliana G, and Serena Chen. Self-Compassion Increases Self-Improvement Motivation. Sage; on behalf of the Society for Personality and Social Psychology, 2012. (Self-Compassion is Key)

Canfield, Jack and Janet Switzer. The Success Principles: How to Get From Where You Are to Where You Want to Be. William Morrow, 2004. (Select Your Purpose)

Carlson, Richard. Don't Sweat the Small Stuff and It's All Small Stuff: Simple Ways to Keep the Little Things From Taking Over Your Life (Don't Sweat the Small Stuff Series). Hyperion, 1996. (When to do nothing)

Cloke, Kenneth and Joan Goldsmith. Resolving Conflicts at Work: Ten Strategies for Everyone on the Job. Jossey-Bass, 2011. (Resolve Conflict)

Clutterbuck, David. Everyone Needs a Mentor: Fostering Talent in Your Organisation. CIPD Publishing, 2004. (e-mentoring)

Deloitte Millennial Survey. www.deloitte.com/MillenialSurvey, January 2014. (Why This Design?)

Deming, W. Edwards. Out of the Crisis. MIT Press, 1986. (Continuous improvement)

Doran, George T. There's a S.M.A.R.T. way to write management's goals and objectives. Management Review, Volume 70, Issue 11(AMA FORUM), pp. 35–36, 1981. (S.M.A.R.T. goals acronym)

Drucker, Peter F. The Practice of Management, 1954. (S.M.A.R.T. goals concept)

Emmons, Robert A. and Michael E. McCullough. Counting blessings versus burdens: An experimental investigation of gratitude and subjective well-being in daily life. Journal of Personality and Social Psychology, Vol 84(2), Feb 2003, 377-389 (Gratitude)

Fredrickson, Barbara L., Michael A. Cohn, [...], and Sandra M. Finkel. Open Hearts Build Lives: Positive Emotions, Induced Through Loving-Kindness Meditation, Build Consequential Personal Resources. J Pers Soc Psychol. Author manuscript; available in PMC Aug 15, 2011. Published in final edited form as: J Pers Soc Psychol. Nov 2008; 95(5): 1045–1062. doi: 10.1037/a0013262 (Attitude of Possibility)

Friedman, Howard S. and Leslie R. Martin. The Longevity Project: Surprising Discoveries for Health and Long Life from the Landmark Eight-Decade Study. 2011 by Hudson Street Press, 2011. (S.M.I.L.E. is Ageless)

Half, Robert. On Hiring. Crown, 1985. (Reflect on Attitude)

Hay, Lousie L. You Can Heal Your Life. Hay House, Inc, 1984. (Affirmations)

Hill, Napoleon and W. Clement Stone. Success Through a Positive Mental Attitude. Prentice-Hall, 1960. (Select Your Attitude)

Holzkamp, Klaus. Grundlegung der Psychologie (Foundations of psychology). Frankfurt am Main: Campus, 1983. (Possibility Zone)

Jeary, Tony. Strategic Acceleration: Succeed at the Speed of Life. Vanguard Press, 2009. (Added Value Support)

Kubzansky, Laura D.; Wright, Rosalind J.; Cohen, Sheldon; Weiss, Scott; and Rosner, Bernard. Breathing Easy: A Prospective Study of Optimism and Pulmonary Function in the Normative Aging Study. 2002. http://repository.cmu.edu/psychology/283. (Attitude of Possiblity)

Kushner, Harold. When Bad Things Happen to Good People. Anchor; Reprint edition, 2004. (Resilience)

Maister, David H., Charles H. Green, and Robert M. Galford. The Trusted Advisor. The Free Press, a Division of Simon & Schuster, Inc., 2001. (What is a Mentor)

Merton, Robert K. Social Theory and Social Structure, Free Press, 1968. (Self-fulfilling Prophecy)

Moeller, Dr. Susan. The World Unplugged research study. http://theworldunplugged.wordpress.com, 2014. (Socal media addiction)

Pareto, Vilfredo. The mind and society: A treatise on general sociology (A. Livingston, Ed.). New York: Dover, 1963, Original work published 1927. (Pareto Principal and The Vital Few)

Shingo, Shigeo. The Sayings of Shigeo Shingo: Key Strategies for Plant Improvement (Japanese Management). Productivity Press, 1987. (Easier, better, faster, and cheaper)

Tamir, Diana and Jason P. Mitchell. Disclosing information about the self is intrinsically rewarding. PNAS 2012, published ahead of print May 7, 2012, doi:10.1073/pnas.1202129109. (Social media addiction)

Tice, Lou. A Better World, a Better You: The Proven Lou Tice "Investment in Excellence" Program. Prentice Hall Trade, 1989. (Everything is a Choice)

Tracy, Brian. Maximum Achievement: Strategies and Skills that Will Unlock Your Hidden Powers to Succeed. Simon and Schuster, 1993. (Live a Balanced Life)

White, Barbara. Harness The Power Of Words In Your Life. Source: Free Articles from ArticlesFactory.com, September 7, 2005. (Possibility Blockers)

Whitman, Meg and Joan O'C Hamilton. The Power of Many. Random House LLC, 2010. (Do the Right Thing)

Wihbey, John. Multitasking, social media and distraction: Research review. http://journalistsresource.org/studies/society/social-media/multitasking-social-media-distraction-what-does-research-say#sthash.FNSGGiOU.dpuf, July 2013. (Focus Brings Clarity)

Ziglar, Zig. See You At The Top. Pelican Publishing Co., 1974. (Select Your Attitude)

INDEX

Added Value Support, 113, 117, 118, 123, 133, 145, 152, 199

Affirmations, 42, 57, 95

Attitude
    Accountability, 58, 61, 66, 72, 73, 87, 96, 99, 138, 147, 151, 204, 208
    Choice, 4, 6, 8, 13, 87, 147
    Gratitude, 67, 69, 70, 71, 72, 74, 75, 77, 78, 79, 87, 191
    Possibility, 33, 34, 48, 49, 51, 52, 53, 54, 57, 75, 87, 89, 92, 98, 109, 153, 161, 204
    Purpose, 14, 16, 32, 87, 92, 93, 98, 109

Balance
    with others, 139
    with self, 136

BHAG, 90

Captain of the World, 149, 159

Change
    Accept, 97, 163
    Acknowledge, 162
    Anticipate, 162
    Embrace, 161, 164, 166, 171

Comfort Zone, 47, 57, 167

conflict, 119, 137, 141, 142, 143, 144, 145, 146, 189, 200

constructive feedback, xviii, xix, 30, 31, 143, 181, 183

Danger Zone, 47

diversity, 153, 157, 158, 159, 192

do nothing, 2, 146, 147

Do the Right Thing, 73, 139, 145, 154, 155, 200

Doer, 16, 18, 90, 93, 140

education and training, 113, 115, 125, 133, 182

effective questions, 117, 118, 120, 145

Elevator Pitch, 124

empowerment, 59

financial goals, 104

FOMO (fear of missing out), 147

generosity, 69, 70

goal management, 91, 94, 103, 111

Grateful Service, 71, 74
    Customer, 72, 73, 74, 76, 77, 86
    Server, 75, 76, 86

imperfection, 47, 54, 135, 137

inclusion, 153, 157, 158, 159

interpersonal skills, 145, 148, 149, 159

knowledge and skills, 45, 115, 173

let it go, 147

mantras, 38

Mentoring
    M.E.N.T.E.E., 183, 193
    M.E.N.T.O.R., 181, 193

Millennial Generation, xvi

Motivation, 58, 60, 87

negative attitude, 2, 3, 21, 34, 199

no surprises, 61, 145

P.L.U.T.O. Communication, 145, 150, 151, 159

pass it on, 69, 70, 86, 87

Pinball Path, 92

positive attitude, 2, 3, 18, 19, 21, 55, 122, 131

Positive Wizard, 48, 49, 55, 108, 152, 153, 167, 180, 192, 199

Possibility Blockers, 33, 34, 35, 37, 57, 87, 162

Possibility Wizard, 33, 49, 57, 199

Possibility Zone, 33, 36, 37, 46, 48, 50, 52, 57, 87, 98, 108, 199

QR code, xvii

RAS, 45, 46, 57, 95, 162, 199

ready-fire-aim, 196

resilience, 60, 69, 99

respond, don't react, 6

responsibility, 59

S.M.I.L.E.
    Action, 195
    Ageless, 196
    Continuous, 198
    Invest in Yourself, 45, 113, 115, 118, 123, 125, 198, 199, 210
    Live a Balanced Life, 30, 105, 135, 136, 137, 143, 155, 158, 159, 200
    Manage Your Goals, 22, 41, 45, 89, 105, 145, 198, 199, 210
    Manage Your Resources, 103
    Select Your Attitude, 1, 40, 45, 87, 89, 113, 140, 145, 152, 153, 198, 199, 210

scotomas, 35

self-talk, 37, 38, 42, 49, 57, 108

setbacks, xviii, 6, 17, 33, 60, 91, 98, 99, 101, 110, 145, 186, 192, 198

Six P's, 22, 91, 111

Smiler, 18

Solver, 20, 30, 31, 124, 125

stop, feel, think, act, 6

Toyota Principle, 98, 111

Uncomfortable Zone, 46, 54, 57, 108, 109, 161, 164, 167

Victor, 23, 24

Visualization, 39, 57, 98

Your People, xviii

ABOUT THE AUTHOR

Award-winning business consultant and sales and marketing expert, Jim Dreher has over thirty years of experience in a rapidly changing industry. He has authored hundreds of sales, marketing, and technical publications, and self-published five smartphone apps. Currently working in Hewlett-Packard's Technology Services Division, he helps customers solve their Information Technology problems by designing lifecycle solutions. Jim holds undergraduate degrees in Technology and Business Management, a graduate degree in Project Management, and is a certified Project Management Professional, PMP®. He has a unique depth and breadth of experience in computer programming and repair, service delivery management, project management, sales and marketing, and solution architecture. Jim lives in Southern California where he enjoys his family, music, magic, travel, and golf.

For more information, visit our web site:

SmileForSuccessBook.com

Scan to view our Website!

Made in the USA
San Bernardino, CA
10 June 2014